Praise for *Climbing Rejectic*

"Where was this book when I was starting out? Nick Wyman gives the young actor an indispensable roadmap to navigate the 'business of show' and does so with his unique blend of honesty, wit, and boundless compassion."

—Tony Goldwyn

"If only I had had Nick's wise and witty book as reference when I began my theatrical journey! He writes with such humor and humanity, as only he could. This should be on every young actor's must-read list. And Michael has captured the tone so perfectly!"

—Judy Kaye

"As a young actress living in New York, I thankfully got my hands on this book right before two of the biggest meetings of my career. It's the perfect tool to prep you for those career milestones like landing an agent, meeting with producers, joining a union, or picking a school if you're just starting out. Plus, it's the prefect length for a plane ride from NYC to LA. If it wasn't for this book, I'd still be going to open calls rather than agent appointments."

—Loretta Anne Miller

"Nick Wyman's book is as entertaining as it is valuable. *Climbing Rejection Mountain* is filled to the brim with detailed, practical advice on functioning as an actor, written from the perspective of an expert. In sharing stories from his own successful and varied career, Nick imparts wisdom and insight that any actor—and indeed, any working professional—could benefit from. At the same time, each page is filled with wit and humanity. With his decades of experience, and thoughtful intelligence, Nick gives readers an arsenal of specific recommendations on both day-to-day life as an actor and also the bigger picture. The book is a must-read for actors at any stage of their career."

—Jennifer Ashley Tepper

"Nick writes it like he lives it. When climbing mountains, he makes the switchbacks great fun!"

—JEFF MCCARTHY

"Wonderful. Full of really helpful information! It's a terrific handbook for both the aspiring actor and inspiration for anyone in the business who wants to remember why they are there. Really useful! AND entertaining. It's given me a lot to think about, and I'm out of the game! I wish I'd had something as clear as this when I was starting out."

—DANA IVEY

Climbing Rejection Mountain

Climbing Rejection Mountain

An Actor's Path to Success, Stability & Self-Esteem

Nick Wyman

Illustrated by **Michael X. Martin**

APPLAUSE
THEATRE & CINEMA BOOKS
Guilford, Connecticut

Published by Applause Theatre & Cinema Books
An imprint of The Rowman & Littlefield Publishing Group, Inc.
4501 Forbes Blvd., Ste. 200
Lanham, MD 20706
www.rowman.com

Distributed by NATIONAL BOOK NETWORK

Credits for images are listed on page 195, which constitutes an extension of this copyright page.

The author thanks *Equity News* for permission to reprint his previously published pieces, "Why I Do Theatre," "Mosaic," "To Join or Not to Join? My Rejoinder," "You Have a Dream," and "Working All the Time."

Library of Congress Cataloging-in-Publication Data available

ISBN 978-1-4930-5165-6 (paperback)
ISBN 978-1-4930-5166-3 (e-book)

♾ The paper used in this publication meets the minimum requirements of American National Standard for Information Sciences—Permanence of Paper for Printed Library Materials, ANSI/NISO Z39.48-1992

Contents

Preface .... *viii*

1. Before You Begin 1
   A Cautionary Tale 1
   Should You Be an Actor? 3
   Why Do You Want to Be an Actor? 4
   What Are the Odds? 6

2. Learning the Ropes (and Pitons and Harnesses and . . .) 9
   Training and Education 9

3. Mapping Your Route 15
   NY vs. LA (vs. Chicago vs. Seattle) 15
      "Go West, Young Man!" (or Maybe Go East) 15
      A New York Actor 16
      "Why I Do Theatre" 17
      Tackling the Big City 22

4. Setting Up Base Camp 27
   Survival Jobs and Day Jobs 27
      "Mosaic" 29
   "Know Your Product"—Socrates 32
      A Climber Prepares 32
      Know Who You Are (or At Least Who You Seem to Be) 32
      Your Body, Your Voice 36
      The Four Questions 38
   Your Family, Your Team, Your Karass 44
      The Connection Card 44

A Family Business: from Granfalloon to Karass 51

Building a Family 52

Your Team, Your Network (Network, Network) 54

5. Outfitting Yourself: The Tools of the Trade 57

Headshots 58

Wyman Through the Years.. 58

Picking a Photographer, Picking a Look.................................... 66

Résumés 71

The Union(s) 80

"To Join or Not to Join: My Rejoinder" 81

Where to Find Work Opportunities 83

6. Beginning the Climb... 87

Looking for Work 87

Auditions 87

Monologues 88

Acting in the Audition 91

Audition Songs... 94

In the Audition Room 98

Letting Go of Your Auditions 103

TV and Radio Commercials... 105

7. Sherpas, Guides, and Trail Masters 109

Representation and Representing 109

Finding an Agent 109

In the Room with the Agent... 121

Marketing Yourself/Self-Promotion 124

Your Web Presence/Your Brand 134

Your Website 137

8. The Mental Climb **141**

The Mindset of Success 141

Self-Esteem 141

Tenacity 146

Reviews, Critics, and Other People's Opinions 149

How to Deal with Success.. 151

Doing a Long Run 151

Plays Well with Others 156

Perspective and Comparisons 158

"You Have a Dream" 160

"Working All the Time" 162

9. Choosing, Changing, Creating Your Path........................... **165**

The Power of No 165

The Work You Want to Do vs. the Path of Least Resistance 165

Why *Not* to Do a Job 167

Prince of Broadway 168

The Five Insufficient "*C's*" (C What I Did There?).................... 172

Creating Your Path 174

Taking the Long View/Visualization.................................... 174

Other Sources of Strength, Stability, and Self-Esteem 177

Changing Your Path.. 180

Why Am I Here? 180

What Else Might I Do? 181

Another Mountaintop... 182

10. Your Mountaintop.. **187**

Index *189*

Preface

Climbing mountains is hard. I don't know that from first-hand experience, but I imagine it is—and as a successful actor, I am handsomely paid for my ability to create truth out of imaginary circumstances. Becoming a successful actor is also hard, and that I *do* know from first-hand experience. To climb a mountain, it helps to have the proper tools and equipment, trusted colleagues, training, experience, guides, support systems, and so forth. The same holds for becoming a successful actor.

This book is a guide to being an actor. It is not a "how to" book, at least in the sense of how to act. And it certainly is not *Acting for Dummies*. (Dummies, by that or any more sensitive nomenclature, are unlikely to make good actors. Most good actors I know are quite intelligent.) This book offers my thoughts on how to be or become an actor and how to maintain your sanity, serenity, and sense of self-worth while doing so. Included in these thoughts are some tips that may make you a successful actor—but (spoiler alert) the odds are wildly against you.

Whether you are just beginning to contemplate a career as an actor or you are at the base camp and ready to begin your ascent or you are already on the path or even on the upper slopes of the mountain, I think you will find useful advice in these pages. It is a collection of my ideas and points of view. They are not Gospel; they are not The Way. They are a reflection of what has worked for me and what I have learned. Take what you like and leave the rest.

1
Before You Begin

A Cautionary Tale

Once upon a time, a young innocent came to the Big City.

He was ignorant, which he hated. He was insecure, which he hated. He was unaccomplished, which he hated.

He didn't know anyone—or didn't think he knew anyone—in Show Business, and he spent little time trying to explore or remedy that.

Without consulting anyone, he found a photographer to take his first headshot. Again without consultation, he chose his look: blond bangs/wispy mustache, and dressed in a black turtleneck against a black background—yielding a photograph of a disembodied head of dubious employability.

He stood in endless lines to audition for shows without a clear idea of what they were looking for. At a chorus call for sophisticated, soigné dancer-singers for *Irene*, he belted out 32 bars of "The Pirate King" from *Pirates of Penzance*.

When he made connections with people who actually had a place in the world of Show Business, he didn't spend any time maintaining or strengthening those connections.

He turned down jobs he was offered—national tours, pre-Broadway tours, regional theatre—and never wrote the directors or casting agents a note of explanation or apology.

He made no concerted effort to save money or create a rainy-day fund.

He made mistake after mistake.

But . . .

He learned from his mistakes.

He figured out what worked—and what didn't.

He created a network of supportive friends and professionals.

He went on to make millions of dollars working as an actor in all areas of Show Business.

He became well-known, well-respected, and perhaps even more important, comfortable in his own skin.

That young innocent, of course, was . . . Seth Rogen.

No, it was Nick Wyman, and it is my fervent wish that this book may mitigate some of your ignorance and insecurity and perhaps put you on the path to accomplishment—to success in both life and acting.

Should You Be an Actor?

Perhaps with a few pointed inquiries we can get you your money back on this book or at least save you from years of misguided toil.

How much do you want to be an actor? The critical response is "A lot!" or "More than anything!" If you answer "Sort of," or "A bit," or "I don't know," that's a prime indicator that the acting life is not for you.

The usual advice proffered to those considering an acting career is, "If there's something else you think you might like to do, do that. But if you have a strong desire to be an actor, go for it." People frequently say, "If you really want to be an actor, don't let anybody talk you out of it." I say, "If anybody can talk you out of it, you're not going to be an actor." Because people will try to talk you out of it. The Business itself will try to talk you out of it.

Often, acting seems like a never-ending stream of rejection. No is the default setting. And this makes a certain amount of sense: if 20 people audition for a role, 19 are going to be told no. And sometimes that 20 people is more like 100; that's a lot of nos. And that's not counting as nos all the people who wanted to audition but couldn't get seen.

When Cameron Mackintosh was bringing Andrew Lloyd Webber's massive West End hit *The Phantom of the Opera* to Broadway, thousands of actors aspired to be in the show. Most of those aspirants never even got seen for the show, but the casting office did see hundreds and hundreds of them, probably a hundred or more just for the roles of Firmin and Andre, the two opera house managers. Out of all those nos, I was one of two who got a yes. So, it can be done. I'll tell you more about that later. (I shall repeat this annoying little phrase, a trick to keep you working your way through my prose, so frequently that I shall henceforth merely use ITYMATL. It is an acronym, not a Mayan archaeological site.)

Why Do You Want to Be an Actor?

"I want to be rich and famous."

If you want to be an actor so you can become rich and famous, you are aiming for an infinitesimally small and unlikely target. It's like saying, "I'm going to law school so I can become a US Senator" or I'm joining the Air Force so I can be an astronaut." Yes, some law school grads become senators; yes, some members of the Air Force become astronauts; and yes, some actors become rich and famous. The vast preponderance do not.

"I love the laughter and applause and the acknowledgement of the audience."

I can relate to this one (as can, I think, all actors—perhaps all humans.) An audience is an actor's necessary collaborator in Theatre, and there is a profound satisfaction in moving them to laughter or tears, to eliciting their applause, to winning their approval. It is intoxicating and many performers crave it.

There is perhaps a psychological element to this. In *Chicago*, Fred Ebb writes for Billy Flynn that his clients went onstage "because they never got enough love in their childhood." Whether one got little love or lots of love as a child, it is gratifying to get the approval and appreciation of audiences and critics. But audiences and critics are fickle and fallible: if you live for the bravos, laughs, and applause, you may well die at the silence and indifference. Better to develop self-appreciation and self-esteem—and I'll tell you more about that later (ITYMATL).

"My greatest creative pleasure is in discovering why people behave as they do and representing that behavior truthfully."

I'm not sure I believe you, but that's a pretty swell reason.

"I have the best time working with other people to find the best way to tell a dramatic story."

This is a pretty terrific reason, and it is part of what keeps actors in the Business in the face of modest encouragement and substandard financial remuneration.

My freshman year in college, lured by a flattering recruiting letter that I realized only in retrospect had been sent to everyone of my height in our class, I went out for crew. It was arduous training (running up and down the steps of the stadium with a 50-pound sandbag slung around my neck) and a difficult sport to master. I was generally terrible; I would get off rhythm and hit the guy ahead of me in the back with my oar handle. However, when it was working and I was in sync with the other guys and our coxswain—it was magical. The boat would literally skim along the Charles River in proof of the expression "the sum is greater than its parts." It was rare (for me) and enormously gratifying.

Acting frequently gives me that same gratification: being "a part of," contributing to a greater-than-myself enterprise, whether in a small or a large way.

"There is nothing else I love to do as much as acting. I can't think of anything else I would be happy doing."

This is a powerful statement and will stand you in good stead when the Business begins assaulting you with rejections. Commitment is as strong a predictor of success in acting as it is in a marriage. "Well, if he/she doesn't work out, I can always get a divorce" is a likely precursor to that divorce; "If I'm not making $100K in two years, I can always sell insurance" is a sure path to selling insurance.

There is nothing wrong with selling insurance (just as there is nothing wrong with acting). Non-acting jobs are not only okay, they are usually necessary to supplement an actor's income. Part of being an actor, for almost every actor, is doing something else as well.

What Are the Odds?

Let's say you have come up with a successful satisfying answer to "why do you want to be an actor?" Now let's take a look at the odds against you.

There are 51,000 members in Actors' Equity, the stage actors' union, and 160,000 members in SAG-AFTRA, the screen actors' union. Allowing for overlap, that's 180,000 professional actors or about 4,000 actors in every single-year age cohort between 20 and 65: 4,000 professional 20-year-olds, 4000 professional 21-year-olds, and so forth.

If you are in high school and you hope to be a professional actor, you are undoubtedly among the better actors in your high school. Let's give you the benefit of the doubt and call you the best actor or actress in your high school. (But even if you are arguably the second or third best, don't lose heart. Talent is only part of what determines your success as an actor.) There are 91,947 high schools in the US. That's 180,000 best actors/actresses graduating every year. Eliminate 20,000 for single-sex schools and you have 160,000 exemplars. Imagine that one in four—no, one in *ten*—manage to convince their parents to allow them to pursue an acting career. That is 16,000 best actors and actresses each year pursuing approximately 4,000 union memberships. The odds are at least three to one against you. And that doesn't count the young actors flooding NY and LA from Canada, Britain, Australia, and elsewhere. And union membership, while an invaluable hallmark of success and a necessary part of an acting career (ITYMATL), is no guarantee of earning a living as an actor. Most Equity and SAG-AFTRA members do something else to pay part of (or all of) their bills.

So, the odds are definitely against you. Going by the odds, you are unlikely to earn a union card. You are very unlikely to earn your living as an actor. Sigh. But—*but*—the Business always needs new young people, and some people your age are indeed going to get that union card, and some are actually going to be successful actors. This book is designed to tilt the odds a little bit in your favor.

And if you do indeed want to be a professional actor, pursue it with a fierce, unwavering commitment and with every ounce of your passion and ability. If you do, one of two things will happen: either you will become a successful professional actor or you will discover some other career path. And whichever result occurs, you will be saved from becoming a regretful 50-year-old saying, "Maybe I should have . . ." "What if I had . . ." or "I wish I had tried . . ."

2
Learning the Ropes (and Pitons and Harnesses and . . .)

Training and Education

The training of an actor used to follow a process similar to the training of a silversmith or a cabinet-maker or other craftsman/tradesman: you learned by observing and then by doing, beginning as an apprentice, becoming a journeyman, and eventually earning full status. Young actors carried the spears and filled the crowd scenes in acting companies, graduating to small roles and eventually finding their place in the company as an ingenue or character man or soubrette or comic or juvenile or leading man or leading lady. (Roger Rees used to talk about his initial four years of "mime training" with the Royal Shakespeare Company before they entrusted him with lines, let alone a significant role.) Acting was a trade, a craft that you learned by doing, by participating in the trade, by observing other craftsmen.

Now acting is often characterized as a profession—not a bad thing—and many people receive training for this profession at conservatories and universities. Sometimes this university training can cost the prospective actor a couple hundred thousand dollars. That's a lot of money to spend for what the odds say is an unlikely shot at even modest success.

There are many, many different programs in which to receive professional training and many different paths to follow. You can go to a nonacademic training program right out of high school (American Academy of Dramatic Arts, the American Musical and Dramatic Academy (AMDA), Circle-in-the-Square, National Theatre Institute (NTI) at the O'Neill Theatre Center). You can go to a conservatory for a BFA (Boston Conservatory, North Carolina School of the Arts, Juilliard School, SUNY Purchase, University of Cincinnati—College Conservatory of Music.) You can go to a university for a BFA in drama or musical theatre (Carnegie Mellon, NYU Tisch, Michigan, Ithaca, Northwestern, Point Park University, University of the Arts, Emerson). You can go to college for an academic BA and then go to a graduate program (Yale, Juilliard, Florida State) or one of the above nonacademic training programs. You can study at a program linked to a regional theatre (ACT in San Francisco, Trinity Rep/Brown in Providence, Asolo Rep/FSU in Sarasota, the Guthrie). You can attend a summer instructional program (NTI and others). You can work as an apprentice at a summer theatre (Williamstown, Barrington Stage, Berkshire Theatre Festival). You can go to London and do undergraduate training or graduate training or a summer program at RADA or LAMDA or Guildhall or Central School or the Drama Centre.

You can create your own training program in NY or LA or elsewhere after you go to college (whether you major in drama or something else) or straight from high school. There are lots of fabulous scene study classes, voice teachers, dance classes, and so forth. Do some research, get some recommendations, take a sample class or two if possible.

There are a myriad of possible approaches to training, and the good news/ bad news is that any one of them might be the right one for you and none of them is the right one for everyone. Just as there is no one right way to perform a role, there is no one right way to approach that role and no one right way to teach acting. You need to find something that is useful that makes sense to you, that resonates with you, that fits with where you are in your life and what you are trying to achieve.

Coming out of high school you will have a hard time figuring out which school/program has the best acting teacher or, at least, the best one for you. The first step is choosing among nonacademic, conservatory, full academic, or create-your-own. Which one of those suits your abilities, strengths, and aspirations best? A second step deals with the three most important words to your success: network, network, network.

People feel a connection to their school and consequently their fellow alumni and are likely to give a fellow grad a hand up. There is a Facebook group called the Michigan MT (Musical Theatre) Mafia with 158 members. In the early and mid-'70s, Joe Papp produced playwrights from the Yale Drama School and hired directors from Yale as well. They, of course, used those actors with whose work they were most familiar—their fellow Yale Drama classmates.

Many schools have a long history of successful professional graduates (Northwestern, Carnegie-Mellon, Juilliard), but other schools with several notable graduates have popped up (Ithaca, Elon, Baldwin Wallace). You can either trade on a long-established tradition or help create a new one.

My two primary pieces of advice for training and education are: 1) get as much experience as you can, and 2) get an education. Few things will teach you as much about acting and how you need to approach it as performing in front of an audience. Do plays, musicals, dance pieces—get in front of an audience. A full-fledged production is best, but even doing scenes in front of your fellow students in a scene-study class is good. An audience teaches you so much about what works and what doesn't.

I am also a big fan of an academic education for two reasons. First, as I said in my intro, good actors are no dummies. They are not only smart, they are educated. Admittedly a number of actors are not college educated, but they tend to be widely read autodidacts. When you are trying to understand a script or a scene, the broader and deeper your background, the more points of reference you have the better. And most directors speak out of their rational, educated mind; the more educated your rational mind is, the more points of connection you will have to enable you to translate the director's intellectual advice into something your heart, gut, and emotions can use.

Second, remember that the odds are stacked heavily against you. It well may be, despite your talent and tenacity and my brilliant counsel, that several years into your efforts at a career you will find yourself at a crossroads. At this crossroads you may decide that the acting business is too much stress, too little remuneration, too much insecurity, or too little fun—or all those things. If so, it will be really useful to have a college degree (and preferably not a BFA from a conservatory) with which to pursue your next life goals.

Now take this with a grain of salt and consider the source. I am recommending what I am most familiar with because I went to an academic college (Harvard) and didn't initiate any formal acting training until after I graduated. But even though this Harvard undergrad was focused at the time on an academic career, I spent every summer and all my extracurricular times doing plays and musicals. I was learning acting by doing while I was becoming educated.

There are other factors that go into the equation. Perhaps you are monomaniacally focused on acting and show no particular academic bent. Perhaps you are a gorgeous 18-year-old young woman who is loath to spend four of her most employable years at college. (Though to counterbalance this last argument, I point to Ivy Leaguers Jodie Foster, Natalie Portman, and Emma Watson.)

Another issue is money. Many private colleges and universities charge fifty to sixty thousand dollars a year or over $200K for four years. Most people who set out to be actors will not make $200K in their whole acting careers! Not you, of course, because you have this book. But still, it gives one pause.

3
Mapping Your Route

NY vs. LA (vs. Chicago vs. Seattle)

"Go West, Young Man!" (Or Maybe Go East)

"Should I move to NYC or should I move to LA?" New York and Los Angeles are the two magnetic poles of the acting business in the US, with New York being the center of stage acting and Los Angeles the center of screen acting. There are also a number of television and film jobs in NY and a number of stage opportunities (though generally for little or no pay) in LA.

But there are professional acting opportunities in cities all across the country. Chicago has a thriving theatrical scene and a number of television and film opportunities. Seattle, Philadelphia, San Francisco, and Washington all have numerous professional theatres. Miami, New Orleans, Atlanta, and other cities have film and TV opportunities. (Atlanta in particular has developed into a hub of film and television production.)

Professional actors live in cities all over the US. There are 28 different cities that have at least 100 members of Actors' Equity. Actors may choose a place to live for many reasons beyond career opportunities: to be near family, to take care of aging parents or a sick relative, because of a spouse's job, because of one's own day job, because you grew up in the area, because of the weather, because you went to school there, because of the natural beauty, because of the cultural vibe.

In terms of sheer number of paying jobs and professional opportunities, though, LA and NYC are the places to be. Remember those 16,000 graduates who represent the 10 percent of the best actors? Every year, literally thousands of young people descend upon each city (cue Sondheim's "Another Hundred People") to be professional actors. You won't be alone. As to which one you should choose, that depends upon what sort of acting you want to do, what your strengths and skills are, where you might have a support system, and where you would like to live.

Your decision will be a personal one for you own particular reasons, and you are the only one qualified to make that decision. As an example, I will share my decision and the thinking that led up to it.

A New York Actor

I am an Easterner—born in Maine and raised in the New Jersey suburbs. I was educated in the East; my family lives in the East. I like having four seasons; I am willing to suffer through the extremes of summer and winter to earn those beautiful days of spring and fall. I am a driven guy, a type A personality, often more of a human doing than a human being—I like the pace of New York. (Visiting my mother after she moved to Florida, I ran an errand for her at the drugstore. As I was waiting in the check-out line, the clerk stopped her transaction with the customer ahead of me to have a personal conversation with the customer: my hair instantly burst into flames. I would not do well living in the South.)

New York is the epicenter of US theatre, and I enjoy doing theatre. I wrote a piece about it for the *Equity News*. (I was the National President of the stage actors' union Actors' Equity Association for five years, and during that time, I wrote a monthly column to educate, inspire, support, and inform my fellow members. Here is the first of several columns I will be sharing with you.)

"Why I Do Theatre"

An interviewer last week asked me why I became an actor and why I was doing this show in Albany, NY. The glib answer to the first is that the Harvard English department made it clear they didn't think much of my plans to be an English professor, and the obvious answer to the second is "Hey, who wouldn't jump at the opportunity to spend February and March in Albany?" Much as I like to be glib, I thought I'd drill a little deeper for you.

I am an actor because I enjoy the challenge of creating a character, of figuring out why people do what they do and how best to tell an author's story. I like creating recognizable human behavior, but mostly I like the interaction, the connection with people.

When I do a play, I become part of a family. This family—frequently less dysfunctional than most—works together to tell a story. We develop our characters and our relationships organically in a rehearsal lasting sometimes only a week or two (hello, summer stock!) but usually four, five, or more weeks. I learn about my character, about the play, about myself, and about the other actors. I solve problems: how to get the truth out of a fellow character, how to con another character, how to reassure an anxious juvenile, how to stop boring the rest of the cast. I grow. I grow as an actor and as a person. With luck I am a better actor and a better person at the end of the process.

When I do television or film, rehearsal/development time is measured in minutes, not weeks. Depending on the size of my role, I may get to know either a portion of that television/film family or a tiny portion of that family. Indeed, our interaction is frequently so brief that I never become part of their family; I am an acquaintance, a transient visitor.

The roles I play in these media are usually too small to have an arc in the script; their drive-by relationship with the leading players reflects my family visitor status. Sometimes I just serve up the exposition that the leading players eschew.

I do my scenes two to ten times, focusing primarily on hitting my marks and maintaining continuity with previous takes. Sometimes I feel I've nailed it, sometimes not so much. Whichever way it went, there is never another chance to improve it or try something new: it's done. Sometimes I feel great, only to be disappointed when I see the end result. In *Planes, Trains and Automobiles*, as a lawyer who jacks up the price of allowing Steve Martin to take my cab while John Candy commandeers said cab, I thought my cool, stone-faced smugness in the face of Steve Martin's importuning would be great. Perhaps it was. In the edited movie when Steve Martin talks, you see a close-up of Steve Martin, not my reaction. Indeed, half the time when Nick Wyman talks, you see Steve Martin's face. The ticket buyers were coming to see Steve, not Nick.

This brings me back to the idea of acting as interacting with people. In the theatre, if I am onstage, an audience member has the option to ignore the good acting and focus on my cheap and vulgar histrionics. When I do movies or television, I have no control over whether the audience gets to see my performance. Indeed, I have no relationship with the audience what-soever—and vice versa. I have no idea whether they love what I am doing or if they can't stand it; and no matter how excited or bored or moved the audience gets, my performance never alters.

Theatre is Community (one of the Five C's; ITYMATL)—and not just the family that puts a theatre piece together. There is community between those of us who do it and those for whom we are doing it. It is actually a collabora-tive effort. We get constant feedback with laughter, applause, and that most precious of audience reactions, utter breath-holding silence.

That immediate reward is very gratifying. Television and film have their rewards as well, and I am always very happy when those rewards come in the mail. I am a big fan of making money with my acting, and theatre is rarely as financially rewarding as TV and film. But just like the rest of you, I didn't go into this business to make money. At the end of my life, the important tally will not be how much money I made but rather how many lives I improved or eased with laughter, with entertainment, with connection. And that's why I do theatre.

A template called the Five *C*'s refers to how I evaluate job possibilities. In generally descending order of importance, these five are Cash (will it bring me substantial sums of money?), Career (will it raise my profile, balance my résumé and/or move me along in my career?), Creative (will this role feed my artistic soul?), Coverage (will this show give me needed weeks for health coverage?), and Community (is this a chance to act with my friends or be of service to the folks I like?) I have taken jobs for each of these five reasons.

Despite what I wrote for the *Equity News*, my motives in doing theatre are not purely humanitarian—there's a mercenary streak in there as well. My skill set serves me well in making money onstage, which is not that easy to do. My ability to make money doing theatre has absolutely influenced my decisions to live in NY and to continue living in NY.

I am not doctrinaire about these choices. In the early 1980s, I played Bruce in Christopher Durang's *Beyond Therapy* at Washington, DC's Arena Stage and Orsino in *Twelfth Night* at the Guthrie Theatre in Minneapolis. I had a great time with both shows and both theatres, and each time I came back to my actress wife Beth and made the pitch that we should buy a house in the suburbs outside DC or Minneapolis and settle down to do great theatre with great people. Each time Beth opted that we stay put and pursue NY careers. If you are part of a couple, where your partner wants to live and/ or work may well be the deciding factor in where you pursue your career. ITYMATL.

I have also made a few extended forays to Los Angeles to investigate the possibility of becoming an LA actor. In 1981 I spent a couple months in LA singing Rex Harrison's costume change music as Freddy Eynsford-Hill in the pre-Broadway tour of the revival of *My Fair Lady*. In 1986 I came out to LA for pilot season.

("Pilot season"—like "grease paint" and "VHS tapes"—is a charming relic of the last century. Once upon a time, there were three major television networks on which everyone watched scripted TV series—sitcoms and dramas. The networks would commission initial episodes or "pilots" of prospective series, and they would cast and film many of these pilots in the first two or three months of the year (pilot season) before choosing in May the most likely pilots to film that summer for the new TV season in the fall. Since an actor's life might be changed forever by being cast in a successful show, and since being cast in a pilot (even one that didn't get picked up by the network) would bring one a nice five-figure salary, many actors migrated from NY to LA for the months of January, February, and March in the hopes of landing a pilot. Nowadays, with scripted TV shows on dozens of cable channels and streaming services, shot in various locations, and initially aired at widely varying times of year, the concentration of pilot season has been watered down.)

I didn't book a pilot—or even a TV commercial as I recall. I spent several pleasant months in a rented home in Westwood: making connections, looking for work, seeing LA friends, and playing with my three-and-a-half-year-old daughter and her My Little Ponies.

Five years later, as the imminent arrival of our third child presaged our displacement from our two-bedroom NY apartment, I went back out to LA to see once and for all if I wanted to be an LA actor or a NY actor in suburbia. To do so, I abandoned the world premiere of Sondheim's *Assassins* directed by Jerry Zaks two weeks into rehearsal. That may not have been a smart career move. Regarding turning down work and leaving jobs? ITYMATL.

Whether it unsettled my career or not, this sojourn in LA settled my mind about LA. If someone had cast me in a hit TV series, I would have happily moved there in a flash. As it was, I got no significant work. Los Angeles somehow crystallizes the lottery aspect of the Business. You can move to LA and become literally world famous in six months. Or you can move to LA and sit on your butt for 20 years. (The joke is that you fall asleep by your pool and when you wake up, you're sixty.) Rather than bet on the six-months-world-famous lottery, I chose to stay in New York.

My reasons were varied: a) I was known in NY; casting directors knew my work, b) I was good at doing what NYC paid actors to do: musical comedy and television commercials, c) there were decent public schools for my kids to be found in the NY suburbs, and d) there was a broader base to the business and cultural environment of NY. (LA is a bit of a company town; it is dominated by the entertainment industry, whereas NY, in addition to its importance to the entertainment industry, is the center of publishing, finance, fashion, and advertising, among other industries.)

So that is why I am a NY actor and not an LA actor—or a Chicago actor or a Seattle actor. You will have other factors in your choice. If you are a fabulous singer/dancer, then Broadway is your likely destination. If you are drop-dead gorgeous, Hollywood will be happy to see you. (New York used to accommodate the drop-dead gorgeous people with a dozen soap operas, but soap operas have gone the way of pilot season.) If you have industry connections, family friends or, heaven help us, a job in another city, that will guide you there.

Tackling the Big City

If the Business can seem like an unclimbable mountain of rejection, New York and Los Angeles (or Chicago or Boston or Washington or Seattle or any other big, strange city) can seem like some impenetrable thicket around that mountain. As a NY actor, I will speak to the difficulties of the Big Apple, but the same ideas apply to LA and elsewhere.

Before you arrive in the city—or immediately thereafter—you need to find a place to live and a survival job. If you were smart enough to be born into a wealthy family, bravo: your work will be much easier. If you are like most of us, you will come smack up against the horrifying cost of rents in NY and LA and many other cities. The good news is that you won't be alone: thousands and thousands of other young adults, many of them aspiring actors, will be in the same boat. The bad news is that you won't be alone. You won't be the only one hunting for a cheap apartment in a decent location. There will be thousands and thousands of other young adults hunting right alongside you.

On a short-term or temporary basis, you can couch surf with friends or relatives. You can track down a short-term sublet through AirBnB or Craigslist or from some other website or some bulletin board. To find a longer-term rental, you can use these options or you can go old school and try newspaper listings or a realtor.

Just as the mantra of the Wyman method is network, network, network, rule no.1 of real estate is location, location, location. In New York City, *the* location has always been Manhattan. In recent years, though, Brooklyn has acquired a hipster cachet that is sort of a combination of Greenwich Village and the East Village.

When I moved to New York City in the early '70s, most actors lived in what was then practically an actors' ghetto—the Upper West Side of Manhattan in the west seventies and eighties. North of 86th Street was a little dicey. North of 96th Street was a serious test of risk tolerance. Some actors lived in Hell's Kitchen (the area in the forties and lower fifties west of the Theatre District, now sanitized by real estate interests as "Clinton"), but that was slightly more dangerous and depressing.

Nowadays, a living situation anywhere in Manhattan is highly sought after. The actors' enclave has migrated up the West Side to the top of Manhattan: Inwood and the area of Washington Heights north of the George Washington Bridge. Astoria in Queens is another area popular with actors. What both these areas have in common is simple and direct subway access to the Theatre District: the N, Q, and R from Astoria, and the A and 1 from Washington Heights.

So, easy access to a Times Square subway line is something to look for. Safety is a key criterion. The Bronx, Brooklyn, Queens, and even Manhattan all have their tough neighborhoods. Clearly, the safest, nicest, most accessible neighborhoods have the highest rents, and the roughest, most dangerous, most inconvenient neighborhoods have the lowest rents, so the question is how much safety and convenience are you willing to trade to save some money? Just as the universe heads towards entropy, most of New York City heads towards gentrification. The tricky part is trying to figure out how fast the process is occurring in any given neighborhood. Once you've made your best guess there, you need to decide how much of a pioneer you are comfortable in being. What's the walk like to the subway? What's that walk like at 11:00 p.m.? Or 1:00 a.m.?

A roommate (or two or three) is a way to leverage your financial strength. A two-bedroom split three ways will surely be cheaper than a one-bedroom on your own. So how much space do you need, and how important is your alone time and your privacy? I shared a three-bedroom apartment (well, two bedrooms and a maid's room) with a drama school classmate, a college classmate, and eventually the latter's girlfriend on the Upper West Side for three years, and we are still the best of friends all these decades later. I think I would have been less happy living on my own.

Figuring out where to live in LA presents slightly different challenges. Whereas the Business in NYC is clearly centered in midtown Manhattan (although there is certainly theatrical activity in Greenwich Village, the East Village, and Brooklyn), the Business is spread out all over greater Los Angeles. There is theatre not only in downtown LA and Hollywood, but all the way from Santa Monica to Pasadena, from the NoHo Arts District and elsewhere in the San Fernando Valley to Costa Mesa. There are studios in Hollywood, Culver City, Century City, Burbank, and elsewhere. There are casting offices all over Los Angeles. No matter where you live, you are going to spend a lot of time driving to other places.

So in Los Angeles, you'll need a dependable car. (Having a car in NYC is not a necessity; in fact, having a car in NYC condemns you to participating in alternate-side-of-the-street parking—NY's answer to the Hunger Games.) Since, as an Angeleno, you will spend so much time in your car, you may want more than a merely dependable vehicle. Although many people in Los Angeles self-identify through their own choice of car and judge others based on what those people drive, I would avoid trying to keep up with the Joneses and paying for more car than you can afford.

Remember, the less you spend on your rent—and in LA, your car—the less you have to make from your survival job to survive. Ideally your rent should not exceed 30% of your take-home pay or 25 percent of your gross pay. (This historical rule of thumb has definitely been bumped up a few percentage points in today's real estate market.) Remember that in addition to such universal necessities as food, shelter, clothing, transportation, and so forth, you will be spending money on your continuing education and training: taking classes and lessons, seeing theatre.

In order to pay for all this, you will need a survival job or day job.

4
Setting Up Base Camp

Survival Jobs and Day Jobs

If you are lucky, the day job is a) financially rewarding, b) enjoyable work, and c) on a flexible/complementary schedule that enables you to audition, rehearse, and perform. There are many, many jobs that actors have chosen, discovered, or created in order to support their acting careers: waiter, cab driver/Uber driver, website designer, proofreader, paralegal, temp, voice teacher, dance instructor, scene coach, accompanist, barista, caterer, bartender, party entertainer, etc. etc.

Knowing your own strengths and skills, you will undoubtedly have additional ideas. Your friends and your family of choice may well have other ideas that you won't have considered. Use your friends and family of choice and the other aspiring actors you meet as a reference: they will have ideas about where to live, about job opportunities. Put it out there. Ask for support, help, information. (And of course, thank those who help.)

"Acting is my passion. I won the Irene Ryan Award in college, then I got a partial
scholarship to Carnegie-Mellon. I just found this dude who does headshots for
$60, and I scored this sweet share situation in Inwood. I'm also freelancing with an
awesome commercial agent, I got a callback to understudy Tybalt at The Public,
and my acting coach is the guy who works with the guy in the TWILIGHT movies.
Anyway, while you guys are looking over the menu, I'll go get your drinks."

Here's a column I wrote for the *Equity News*:

"Mosaic"

I ran into one of my fellow tall, blond *Die Hard* thugs last week, and in an exchange of "How ya doin's?" he rather shamefacedly admitted that not only had he not done any more big-budget feature films, he'd just been doing a little of this, a little of that. "Hey, it's a mosaic," I said. *Mosaic* is my second-favorite metaphor for our theatrical life. As an actor, our professional lives are far from the 50-years-and-a-gold-watch sort of single-employer career (although the fellow who replaced me in *Phantom*—I can't reveal his name, but his initials are George Lee Andrews—is at 22 years and counting). The good news/bad news of our vocation choice is that no one job lasts too long. We need to put together a mosaic of jobs to create a livelihood.

Some of the pieces in our mosaic are big and bright: national tours, classy LORT productions; and some are smaller: readings, waiver productions. Some pieces are from the domains of our sister unions: television, radio, film, audiobooks, opera. Some pieces are from yet-to-be-organized arenas: cruises, European tours. And some pieces are from our non-acting work: waiting tables, word processing, bartending.

A buddy of mine with whom I have shared a NYC stage responded to my website column on voting by admitting that he hadn't voted. He's worked on Broadway, and he's done leads in LORT, but he's only worked seven weeks in the last year and a half, and he feels "disconnected" from the union and the Business.

The union is not a snooty club for the constantly working; it is an association constituted "to advance, promote, foster, and benefit all those connected with the art of the theatre." We all have a stake in the Business, an equitable stake. We're all in this together; sometimes we're working, sometimes we're not. Since there are more good stage actors than good stage jobs, for most of us the nonworking times outnumber the working times. To fill out our livelihood mosaic, we need to look for nonstage work and non-acting work. This is par for the course and no reason to feel disconnected or distant from AEA. And indeed, our livelihood mosaic is just part of our life mosaic, fitted among the pieces for family, friends, hobbies, exercise, service, religion, community.

The beauty or value of your life's mosaic has nothing to do with the size or number of the Equity pieces; they are just part of a much bigger picture. Know, however, that your elected leadership and your union staff are working to develop as many new mosaic pieces as they can and to make existing ones larger (i.e., more remunerative) and that you, whether you have been working a lot or a little, are part of Equity's mosaic. You are family—and that's my favorite metaphor for our theatrical life.

Everyone on this planet has to put together the mosaic of their life. For many people, the job parts of that mosaic are a single large, unchanging piece. That is not the case with actors. For all actors, the acting pieces change. For most actors, the job pieces are some acting pieces and many nonacting pieces. These nonacting pieces are usually essential to pay for rent, food, clothing, classes, and so forth.

Remember that even for those fortunate few who are able to make their entire livings through performing, their employment is also a mosaic. Professional acting is not forty hours a week for forty years at the same job site. I sometimes have forty different jobs in the same year. The hope is that all the jobs—whether performing jobs or otherwise—add up to enough money to pay the bills.

If not, don't be shy about asking your parents for help. It can take a while to figure out how to make ends meet, particularly if you have some serious student debt. ITYMATL. If your folks are well off, huzzah! I often say—with only a smidgeon of irony—that one of the best preparations for an acting career is a trust fund. I have known a number of successful actors whose early acting struggles were cushioned by their family money.

But however successful you or your family are financially, remember that work—whether acting or nonacting—is only part of the mosaic. Family, friends, love, community, and service are equally or more important. The Business, even for the most successful, is so difficult and so strewn with disappointment and rejection that you need other sources of strength and stability to support you. ITYMATL.

"Know Your Product"—Socrates

A Climber Prepares

Given that the odds are wildly against you ever earning your living as an actor, how can you help improve those odds? There are things you can do before you ever go into your first audition, and there are things you can do while you are actively looking for work.

An Actor Prepares. I have to confess: I have never read this Stanislavsky book. Maybe I'm lazy. Partially it is that I believe in doing, not in reading about doing. (My Unitarian friends say that the definition of a Unitarian is someone who, given a choice between heaven and a lecture on heaven, chooses the lecture.) But I do believe you should prepare. And I definitely believe you should read *this* book about preparing and doing.

Know Who You Are (Or at Least Who You Seem to Be)

The first part of preparation is knowing where you are, where you are starting from, who you are, what you've got to work with. Do an honest, thorough self-examination, an inventory of your strengths and weaknesses, your mad skills and your more problematic areas. Try to stay away from, or at least not linger on, judgement of yourself as a person—particularly on some good/bad scale.

For instance, are you tall or short? I am tall—excessively tall, some might say: 6'5" for most of my adult life. Sometimes it has worked in my favor: the tall, bossy husband in *Very Good Eddie*, the leader of a group of tall Aryan henchmen in *Die Hard with a Vengeance*. Sometimes it has worked against me. Very early in my career, I auditioned to replace the actor playing Starbuck in a successful off-Broadway production of *110 in the Shade*. The audition was on their stage, a raised platform set up in a ballroom of the old Hotel Dixie on 42nd Street. I got a call from them that night thanking me and telling me that I was the best person they had seen that day, but—I was just too tall for them to light. (Cue: sad trombone.)

Similarly, I often use the example of Danny DeVito, whom I saw off-Broadway in *One Flew Over the Cuckoo's Nest* before he became famous. Surely, well-meaning adults had told him, "Danny, you're no glamor puss. You're five feet tall, for Pete's sake. You have no chance in this business." Thankfully, he didn't listen—because his height *works* for him. It makes him very specific—as my height makes me; and just as it is critical in your acting choices, specificity in your look can be a godsend in this business. If a movie director has a character who appears in the beginning of a film and doesn't recur until near the end, and he needs the audience to instantly recognize the character when he reappears, he needs an actor who is very specific, very particular looking.

So, whether you are tall or short, or very tall or very short, it's not good or bad: it's just what's so. It is just part of what makes you "you" and not somebody else. It is what you have to work with.

What else do you have to work with? Are you plump? Portly? Obese? Are you slender? Skinny? Wraith-like? Are you blonde? Brunette? Redhead? Are you Asian? African American? Are you funny? Quick-witted? A total scream? Are you muscular? Or not so much? Are you gorgeous? Or not so much?

A word about beauty. It may have been a joy forever to Keats, but he kicked off at 29 and beauty becomes a lot more difficult in your 30s and 40s. Axiomatically, beauty is also in the eye of the beholder. You may think you're nothing special, and the director or casting director may find you to be a knockout. Or, sadly, vice versa.

The standard of beauty—if there is such a thing—is also different in the theatre than it is on film or television. Many more people can play "beautiful" onstage than onscreen. Acne scars that disappear from the fifth row in a stage production can be problematic when one's face is forty feet high on a movie screen. Relatively plain women have had long stage careers frequently playing beauties.

And just as leading men of modest height may veto taller leading ladies or taller featured men, leading ladies may well be loath to have another woman in the production whose beauty might put them in the shade. So beauty, although it is usually a distinct advantage—particularly for women and particularly in television and film—can sometimes be a hindrance.

In the glory days of soap opera, beauty was about all you needed. As a day player on some soap, I remember watching a gorgeous young male actor who had just been signed to a contract role on the soap opera do his first scene. He was appallingly bad. He didn't have the skills for a seventh-grade class presentation. But he was very good looking.

In a strange way, homeliness can be almost as much of an advantage as beauty. You never have to worry about outshining the star, and in the host of attractive actors, you will stand out. You will have the specificity, the particularity that the director may well be looking for. Steve Buscemi (who is not only a brilliant actor but also one of the nicest guys in Show Business) is a rather odd-looking duck, but he has had an extraordinary career in film and television.

Almost as much of an advantage (and one without any downside) is funny. On his deathbed, the actor Edmund Gwenn acknowledged that his last moments were difficult, "but not as difficult as playing comedy." The writers of *My Favorite Year* turned this into the snappier "Dying is easy; comedy is hard." And there is a certain truth to it. We will all at some point master the art of dying; not everyone can master the art of comedy. However, if you, as they say, can "do funny," you have a huge leg up on other people.

There are many components to comic acting: Timing. Inflection. Focus and misdirection. Facial expressions or lack thereof (deadpan). Takes. Double takes. Physical comedy. Slapstick. Prop comedy (Lazzi). Shticklak. And on and on.

There are many different ways to do funny, as you may gather either from watching a particularly inventive colleague try various approaches to make a line or scene work, or from watching an actor and director debate how best to get the laugh. Getting the laugh is often the objective, and a good comic actor knows how to do it while still telling the story and without destroying the suspension of disbelief. Most good comic actors will have a similar approach to getting the laugh. What separates a great comic actor from a good one is his or her surprising/unexpected approach to the line or scene.

I personally think you either can do comedy or you can't. Since the journey of a professional actor usually begins with funny bits to amuse his or her parents and progresses to becoming the class clown, most actors have a taste and a talent for comedy. If you are not sure about your comic chops or you want to improve them, study with improv comedy troupes such as the Upright Citizens Brigade in NY or LA, Second City in Chicago, or the Groundlings in LA. Or you can simply watch and rewatch performers who make you laugh. Study the masters. (I personally worship at the shrine of Mel Blanc and the Looney Tunes animators.)

Your Body, Your Voice

Prepare your body. Exercise and eat right. Get yourself into your most employable shape. For most of us, that is relatively slender. Remember that the camera, whether or not it adds the proverbial ten pounds, is notoriously unforgiving of whatever extra poundage you yourself may have added.

Not everybody needs to diet and exercise their way to mesomorphic gorgeousness. I did *Whoopee!* on Broadway with Peter Boyden, a wonderful comic actor with a portly physique, and Peter was making a handsome living doing television commercials. Peter's wife was a doctor, and she and Peter's own doctors convinced him that he needed to drop some weight for his health. So Peter did as he was told and dropped dozens of pounds. It may have been the best for his health, but it didn't help his career. The television work dried up, and nonworking Peter was miserable. He gained back the weight.

Genes and heredity are going to play an enormous part in the roles you play and the career you make out of them. In addition to your body type, which you may or may not be able to change; your height; the color of your skin, eyes, and hair; your physical grace and athleticism; your singing voice are all gifts from your parents and forebears. It is your job to make the most of them.

You may, like yours very truly, not be particularly graceful or coordinated, but even a lifetime of being picked last for kickball and softball teams doesn't have to keep you from being picked for a musical with dancing. Take beginning dance classes: jazz, modern, tap. They can only improve your abilities, and they will certainly ease the discomfort of unfamiliarity at dance auditions. You will be used to moving to the music, to hearing people ("And five, six, seven, eight!"); you will be familiar with the terms ("ball change," "shuffle, flap," "second position").

I took dozens of jazz classes in my youth. I even took a couple ballet and tap classes. The end result was more Samuel Johnson's dancing dog than Nijinsky, and I have been the cause of numerous choreographers' drinking problems, but it would have been far worse had I not taken those classes.

As a dancer, I have had some (decidedly modest) triumphs—I did an extended Black Bottom number as Scott Fitzgerald in a 1980 Off-Broadway revue about expatriate writers in 1920s Paris. (Jane Summerhays, as my partner Zelda and my choreographer, deserves a place in heaven for her patience.) I have also had some not-so-triumphant moments. My agent got me an audition for the Gene Kelly role in Broadway's *Singin' in the Rain*. I pointed out to him that I was no tap dancer. "They're looking more for personality," he said. That is how I found myself with 25 dance-capable leading men in a dance

"Hi, everyone! I'm Nicole! Welcome to Advanced Tap!"

studio, repeatedly serving as the humiliatingly incompetent bad example for the assistant choreographer's dance combination. The dance combination (and the job) were so laughably beyond my skill set that I eventually relaxed and just gave in to serving as the goofy audition mascot.

Just as you may not possess terpsichorean genius, you may consider yourself a lousy singer or a nonsinger. Once again, taking a few voice lessons can go a long way toward creating a comfortable and relaxed approach to singing. Today's musical theatre does not require the rafter-rattling voices of Ethel Merman or John Raitt; the ubiquitous wireless personal microphones amplify anyone's voice to fill a theatre.

Even if you don't have a gorgeous voice or an enormous range or if you have limited musicality, you should figure out a song that fits your vocal range (or lack thereof) and musical abilities (or lack thereof) so that you have something to sing at musical auditions. As to specifics about audition songs, ITYMATL.

Voice lessons may not be able to beautify your voice significantly or extend your vocal range enormously, but they might—and they certainly won't hurt. They will also make you more comfortable with singing and with learning a song. You will get a sense of your skills and limitations, and you will improve your musicality. Another way to improve your musicality is to learn an instrument. Piano lessons or guitar lessons or a music theory class at school will all improve your ability to read music and participate in musical theatre. Indeed, with the advent of *Once* and John Doyle productions of *Sweeney Todd* and *Company*, the ability to play an instrument may be key to being cast in a role.

The Four Questions

Breaking into Show Business sometimes seems like breaking into Fort Knox or Mordor or some other impenetrable, forbidding fortress. Gatekeepers, primed and prepped to say *no*, are everywhere. The classic (if slightly inaccurate) saying is, "You can't get an Equity job without an Equity card, and you can't get an Equity card without an Equity job."

Let's face it: the Business is not holding its breath for you to show up. "We have all the actors we need, thank you" is the attitude of the Business. So how do you overcome this supreme indifference?

I have four questions that I ask my prospective acting students:

1. What is your long suit?

This bridge reference (Does anyone under 50 play bridge anymore?) means: What is your strength? What is your most salient quality? What I am looking for is your identifying character type, your persona, the characteristic(s) that people cast you for. You might also consider whether you fit neatly into one of the classic categories of ingenue, juvenile, soubrette, character man, character woman, leading man, leading lady.

My long suit is arrogant figures of authority—jerks in suits, as I call them. I project power, authority, intelligence, entitlement, judgmentalism, wealth. People cast me as bosses, lawyers, CEOs, doctors.

I have played many other types of roles as well, and I like to think of myself as a very versatile actor, able to play naifs, con men, romantic leads, sociopaths, and so forth. You too probably feel with some justification that you have a broad range. ("Hey, in my high school production of *Oklahoma!*, I played Aunt Eller and Jud.") The Business doesn't care. The Business is not a repertory company. It isn't looking for someone who can play both a maternal fount of homespun wisdom and a simmering cauldron of masculine lust and resentment. You may have been brilliant as Sheridan Whiteside in *The Man Who Came to Dinner*: the Business doesn't care. The Business doesn't need a 20-year-old who, with a little shoe polish in his hair, can do a credible impersonation of a 50-year-old curmudgeon; the Business is overflowing with talented 50-year-old character men.

You need to figure out the diamond-hard, sharpest, finest cutting edge of your talent and your persona—because that is what you are going to use to break into the fortress of the Business. You just need to get that first job doing what you do best. You will get noticed. You will make connections. The people who notice you will say, "Hey she was great as the funny best friend in that play; let's use her as the funny best friend in our play." Your connections (director, producer, choreographer) will say, "Hey, she was great as the funny best friend, let's try her as the character young leading lady in our next piece."

Within the walled city of Show Business lie various inner sancta: Broadway, Television, Movies. You will likely need that sharp fine edge of your talent and your persona to break into those as well. My first Broadway show was *Very Good Eddie*, in which I played a tall, bossy, arrogant young Yale graduate. The Yale aspect may have been character work for this Harvard grad, but the rest was just me—just the sharpest edge of my persona. My first television job was a commercial for Ruffles potato chips in which I played a pompous, know-it-all husband. I have gone on to play many different roles on Broadway and on TV, but it was my long suit that got me in the door.

Ask yourself, what are your most defining characteristics? They may be positive ones (openness, cheeriness, friendliness) or more negative (like my judgmentalism and arrogance). Most particularly, how do *other* people see you? Ask your friends. Ask people who don't know you all that well. Directors and casting people will be meeting you for the first time, and they will make a snap judgement of what your type is, who you basically are, and whether you are right for the role they are casting. (If you are really lucky and everything works out, you will endure decades of people deciding you are not right for a role. That's okay. That's their job. Don't do their job for them—ITYMATL.)

2. Who has your career?

Who is the well-known actor—maybe your age but probably several years or even many years older—who plays "your" roles? This person is your type, your persona. He/she may look a lot like you or just a little. Most importantly, if you were famous and/or a few years/many years older, *you* would be playing their roles.

My first year in summer stock, I did a couple roles originated by another tall, blond actor—Ken Howard. Thirty-five years later, we took on the same role: union president. Over the years I have tried to wedge my size 16 persona into the shoes of such actors as Kevin Kline, Victor Garber, Ron Holgate, David Dukes, Ed Herrmann, et al. None of these actors is my doppelganger (that dubious distinction is shared by Max Von Sydow and Fred Gwynne) but they all played one or more Nick Wyman roles at one time.

3. What roles are you hammer-on-the-head-of-the-nail, dead-solid perfect for?

What are the roles that, if you could just figure out a way to get into the audition room, would make you the answer to a casting director's prayer? What are the roles that you were born to play, that you are the best person on the planet to do?

Lately, I seem to be going through a General Harrison Howell in *Kiss Me Kate* phase: auditions, inquiries, job offers. Who is he? A pompous, arrogant, self-centered jerk in a uniform. (A uniform. Not a suit. Ah, that versatile Wyman.)

Twenty-five years ago, I went through a Miles Gloriosus in *Funny Thing* phase. I think I was asked to do it at three different summer theatres, but I turned them all down to stay in town with my family. I had done the role before (Stephen Sondheim even saw me do it at Harvard), and I thought doing it in summer stock wasn't going to do anything for my career or my bank balance. (How do I choose to do or not to do a job? ITYMATL.)

4. What roles would you like to do?

What are your dream roles? These roles might be roles that you are very right for; they could be roles that you are unlikely ever to be offered; they could be roles you would never be offered. There may be something about the arc, the journey of the character that you respond to. It may be the relationship the character has with another character that draws you. It may just be a fun role.

Some of my dream roles are Hamlet, Henry V, John Proctor (*The Crucible*), Jack Tanner (*Man and Superman*), Sweeney Todd, Henry Higgins. Sadly, I have not played any of them on a professional stage (other than an understudy run-through when I briefly covered Higgins in a Broadway revival)—and I am a little long in the tooth for all but Sweeney and Higgins. However, I have worked on almost all of them in scene study class, so I have taken steps to live out my dreams.

This last question—What roles would you like to do?—is part of the motivation and navigation system of your career. In the midst of day-job drudgery and frustrating audition results, it helps to have a vision of what you would like to be doing. Thinking what roles you would like to play—subsidiary peaks you would like to climb—can help keep you on track in your journey to your Personal Mountaintop. ITYMATL.

The first three questions will help you figure out what you are selling, what you have to offer. Know your product. When you meet with a prospective talent agent, as you consider whether or not you want that person to represent you, you want to be sure that you are both selling the same product. If you see yourself as a femme fatale, a sexy vamp, and the agent sees you as the girl next door, that is likely to be an unhappy and unsuccessful relationship.

The more specific you are in your self-assessment, the more likely you are to find an agent aligned with your goals and, whether you have an agent or not, the better your chances are of targeting the right spot at which to attack the Fortress of Show Biz.

"I'm a feisty, funny soubrette. A Jen Cody type. A young Rhea Perlman. I would kill as Sally in *You're a Good Man Charlie Brown* or as Little Sally in *Urinetown*" is specific.

"I like to sing. I'm pretty good at funny stuff, but I think I could do drama too. I don't know if I'm the right person for a leading role" is much less useful.

Keep an eye out for those roles for which you are dead-solid perfect, and then try to get yourself seen for them. But I must say, it can be difficult.

In 1978, Thomas Wolfe's autobiographical novel *Look Homeward, Angel* was adapted as a Broadway musical, *Angel*. The musical centered on the Thomas Wolfe character Eugene Gant and his family, which included his brother Ben Gant and his father W. O. Gant. Now Thomas Wolfe was a Harvard grad and famously tall (he was 6'6" and wrote on top of a refrigerator)—so I thought I had a literal leg up on everyone. Not only that, but the father was being played by my look-alike Fred Gwynne. A no-brainer. A slam-dunk. Right? I couldn't get an audition for either of the Gant boys. In retrospect, this was not a heartbreaking loss: the show was savaged by the critics and closed a week after opening. In further retrospect, I shouldn't have depended on my agents alone; I should have played the connection card. ITYMATL.

In 1996, five or so years after all those summer theatres were throwing the role of Miles Gloriosus at me, a revival of *A Funny Thing Happened on the Way to the Forum* was being mounted on Broadway. I assumed that I would be asked to audition for Miles, and I assumed (because hey, you have to have confidence) that I would get the part. But there were a couple of other job prospects that I was perhaps more interested in, so I held it as sort of a safety school and didn't pursue it, let alone push my agents. Finally, when the casting began to be announced, I called my agents. "Oh, we submitted you for Marcus Lycus, but Nathan wanted Ernie Sabella" (with whom he'd just happily voiced Timon and Pumbaa in *The Lion King*). So, two lessons to be learned: 1) make sure you and your agent are on the same page, and 2) don't assume people know what you're thinking—talk to your agents and ask for what you want.

Your Family, Your Team, Your Karass

The Connection Card

Remember the connection card that I said should have been played to get an audition for *Angel*? (See? I'm not forgetting about these ITYMATL things.) The connection card (or connection cards) is/are perhaps the most important implement in the Tool Kit of Success.

The creative team behind *Angel* was the same team that had created the very successful *Shenandoah*: composer Gary Geld, lyricist Peter Udell, director Philip Rose, and choreographer Robert Tucker. That connection certainly aided Joel Higgins, one of the featured actors from *Shenandoah*, in getting the role of Ben Gant. In 1975, the same year *Shenandoah* opened on Broadway, choreographer Robert Tucker went on to direct and choreograph a new musical called *Cowboy* up at Goodspeed. This musical just so happened to feature a young actor named Nicholas Wyman. (I used to be Nicholas Wyman in the Business. Then I decided I was more Tony Roberts [who used to be Anthony Roberts before he saw the light] than Laurence Olivier, and I changed it to Nick Wyman.) So, I could have reached out to Bob Tucker and asked him to help me be seen for one of the Gant brothers.

Show Business is a people business, and you will meet thousands of people as you make your way up Rejection Mountain. The secret of success in two words? Be nice. Leave a good impression. Not just because you will meet the same people on the way down that you met on the way up, but because those people may be in a position or rise to a position where they can help you. So be nice. Be considerate. Be gracious. Be charming. Be generous. Be responsive. Be attentive. Be all those things. Do all those things. And you should do them not because that's your insincere, two-faced, Machiavellian plan to claw your way to the top (well, not *just* because that's your insincere, two-faced, Machiavellian plan) Do them because doing so will improve your life and make the journey—the impossible dream, the climbing of the mountain—more bearable. Doing nice things for other people does nice things for you.

Celebrate other people's success, even if it was a success you yourself wanted. You know who got the role of Miles Gloriosus in that *Funny Thing* revival? Cris Groenendaal, who had been my fellow opera house manager in the original cast of *Phantom*. Did I sulk? Did I tell everyone I met how I would have been better? No, I congratulated him on his success and cheered him on. Yes, the Business is unbelievably difficult. The dream may indeed seem impossible. But the empowering place to come from is not scarcity but abundance. No matter how important a job may seem, there are other possible jobs. In fact, there are lots of other possible jobs. And as Ralph Richardson philosophically once said about job choices and job disappointments, "You can only take one train from the station."

Here endeth the lesson. Now back to the insincere, two-faced Machiavellian plan.

Remember the three most important words to your success? *Network, network, network.* Remember the connections that attending well-known theatre schools and colleges can bring? Well, you don't have to wait until college or acting school to begin making connections. You may have useful connections through your high school, your hometown, your parents. What show-biz folk are connected to your high school? Your town? Do your parents or anyone else in your family know people in show biz?

Reach out to these people. Be courteous. Be gracious. Praise them and/or their accomplishments. (Here's the dirty not-so-secret secret about show-biz folk: we all have egos; we all worry that we're not quite as great as we'd like to be; we are all willing to believe it if someone tells us we're great.) Make a request.

The request may be simply to be able to email them or phone them again in the future. It may be for a piece of advice. It may be to ask them to forward an email of yours to a colleague of theirs. It may be to ask them if you could treat them to a cup of coffee or a lunch to ask them a few questions. And then—whatever their response—thank them. If you have their mailing address, send them a written thank-you note. (The silver lining to the abandonment of posted letters in favor of emails is that a thank-you note is now as rare and valuable as a Fabergé egg.)

Rinse, repeat.

Praise people, ask them for advice, thank them. Show-biz folk are not only susceptible to praise or even arrant flattery, they also like to proffer advice. And everyone likes to be thanked.

Who do you talk to? The short answer? Talk to everybody. If you can be charming and funny, by all means be charming and funny. If charm and humor are not your long suits, be kind, be generous, be appreciative, be interested. Being interesting is sometimes a good strategy; being interested is always a good strategy. So listen. Many people believe listening is the key to good acting. Not me, of course. I never listen to other actors onstage or look at them: it just throws off my carefully prepared, prepackaged performance. (And if you believe this, you need to check your facetiousness meter.)

So who are you talking to and what is your relationship? You are talking to those above you and below you on the food chain of show biz and you are talking to those on your own level. Be upbeat with all of them; be encouraging to those below, complimentary and acknowledging of those at and above your level. Your relationship is not that of a dismissive critic or a snarky frenemy: you are an appreciative colleague.

When you are just starting out, any connection to the world of Show Business moves you closer to your goal. As you move further along your actor's progress, you can become more focused in your connections. And as you accumulate your connection cards, you can parlay one into another by asking your connection if they would forward an email or if you can reference them in reaching out to another possible connection.

Above all, don't come off as obnoxious or entitled. Be gracious and grate-ful. If you're an organized sort, keep a record of your connections. (Perhaps even a file of actual connection cards!) Actually, whether you're an organized person or not, start a notebook of the folks you meet. Note when and where you connected; note what you asked and/or what they did for you. Note the date. There will be other opportunities for this sort of organization later. There is a website (site.performertrack.com) that will allow you to track all your meetings, auditions, interviews, and so forth—what you wore, what material you performed, who you met, etc. etc.—for a $9.95 monthly sub-scription (which seems a little ongoingly pricey to me). There is a new website from Ned Donovan and Tony Aidan Vo called www.audition.cat.com that is currently in beta testing and that I think looks like a real winner. If you don't want to create your own notebook, you might try Leslie Becker's *The Organized Actor* workbook.

Make as many connections as you can. If a well-known actor/director/producer/choreographer or the like comes to your town, your high school, your college—do your best to meet them. Google what they've done, then praise them/acknowledge them for some accomplishment as you shake their hand and look them in the eye. Thank them. If you only have time for a brief interaction, don't waste it getting a selfie. They won't remember that, but they might remember the polite, appreciative young woman or man who liked their work in "_____" (fill in the blank).

And ask their advice. If "Do you have any advice?" seems too broad and general, narrow the focus of your question to one of the next steps on your journey: "Is there a school or training program that you would recommend?" "Any books you would recommend that I read?" "Any teachers with whom you've studied that you think are excellent?" "Any theatres you would recom-mend interning at?" "Any other suggestions for a good first step on the road to a career?"

You will get lots of different answers. There are probably as many paths to acting success as there are successful actors. But some answers will recur. Take special note of those answers. Also take note of answers that resonate with you, that fire up your brain or heart or gut. As my friends say, take what you like and leave the rest.

When you go off to college or acting school, take a good, hard look at the folks in your acting class. This is your crew. Your gang. Your peeps. Your cohort. Your posse. Your class. There is a famous scene in the film *The Paper Chase* where the brusquely abusive Professor Kingsfield (played ironically enough by the founder of the Juilliard School's Drama Division, John Houseman) says to his first-year law school students, "Look to your left. Look to your right. One of you won't be here next year." If it were a teacher facing first-year students at a drama school, he or she might say, "Look to your left. Look to your right. Look behind you. Look in front of you. One of you is going to make a living in the Business."

Okay, that assessment may seem a little harsh, but the odds are steep. My class at the Circle-in-the-Square had about 20 or 22 students in the first year. Ten of us came back for the second year. I am the only one who lasted in the Business and certainly the only one who made a living from acting. Was I the most talented? Uh, well, maaaaybe. I just turned out to be the most employable, and there are a lot of things that go into that besides talent. ITYMATL.

But there is no law or rule that says that only one student will make it. Maybe six will make it from your class. Maybe ten. Maybe all of you. That is something worth striving for—because the more of you who make it, the more support and validation each of the others receives. The Business is not a zero-sum game. My success does not come at your expense, even if we're the same type, even if we're going up for the same role. Yes, my pal Groenendaal got what I saw as "my" role in *Funny Thing*, but during the year he was cavorting with Nathan Lane and Whoopi Goldberg at the St. James Theatre,

I did a pre-Broadway national tour of *Applause* (which crashed and burned) and then began six glorious years of employment as Thenardier in Broadway's *Les Misérables*. God may indeed open a window when he closes a door; and in my experience, God's house has a lot more windows than doors.

So—champion your classmates. Root for their success. Treat them well. At the end of your training, they will know your work better than anyone. They may become successful actors and be in a position to hear about a casting opportunity for a role that doesn't fit them but does fit you. They might not become successful actors but instead become successful producers or directors or casting agents. (Many, if not most, directors, producers, and casting agents start out as actors.)

The more of your classmates and schoolmates who become successful in the Business, the more of a reputation your school will develop. Instead of getting a blank look when you tell people where you trained, you will get a knowing, appreciative nod. Younger wannabe actors will hear of your school and move it up their list of potential training grounds. Your school will become more competitive and turn out graduates even more likely to succeed. It is a virtuous cycle.

Your classmates are also likelier than your teachers (and avuncular sorts such as yours very truly) to have cutting-edge ideas about how to pursue your training and your career, and to be up-to-date on the latest apps and technology. They will also be going through many of the identical problems, trials, difficulties, crises, and struggles that you are; maybe they have discovered or crafted some solution to these situations.

Similarly, if you have hit upon a solution, don't keep it to yourself. ("Hey, I'm reading this fabulous new book *Climbing Rejection Mountain!*") If you hear about a job opening or a casting opportunity, tell your classmates. Create a hive mind rather than attempting to stoically conquer the Business all by yourself.

Keep in touch with your classmates. They know you well, and if a role shows up on their radar that is right for you, you want them to think of you. And you should think of them. If you hear about a role that is right for you and that is also right for a pal of yours, let your pal know. If they want you, they don't want your pal and you will get the job. If they want your pal, they don't want you and they will hire your pal and you will have done her or him a solid. Life is not a zero-sum game. It is not necessary for someone else to lose for you to win.

Enjoy your training/education. It is—or should be—a safe space. It is a safe space to risk, to fail, to learn. So go ahead, make mistakes. Mistakes are just opportunities to learn. Make bold choices in your acting. What I admire most in acting is believability and boldness. Those actors who can push the envelope of boldness without sacrificing believability are in my personal pantheon.

I love it when an actor surprises me by making an unusual, strong choice. Kevin Kline ricocheting off the train compartment walls in *On the Twentieth Century*. John Malkovich's intensity as Pale in *Burn This* making me concerned about my own safety fifteen rows from the stage. Two moments from *The Producers*: Gary Beach sitting on the lip of the stage a la Judy Garland and Kathy Fitzgerald's hilarious drunk bag lady in the opening number.

This is, to my mind, one of the major differences between acting in high school and acting professionally. In high school, the director of the school play is looking for those who can read lines believably, who can speak the text comfortably without stumbling or stammering. Sometimes—particularly with the boys' roles—the director will just settle for a warm body. Believability is not enough in the professional world, particularly for stage work. You have to make choices. ITYMATL.

Similarly, in musicals, if a high school guy can sing, he is a shoo-in for roles in his school musical. The ability to carry a tune and the ability to be heard across a medium-sized room (or even just one of those two) make him the answer to a musical director's prayer. It is often a shock to those high school stalwarts when they audition for a professional job and hear dozens of guys with strong, beautiful voices. But whether you have a strong, beautiful voice or merely a passable one, remember: even having a gorgeous voice isn't enough. You have to make choices, you have to act the song, you have to tell a story.

A Family Business: from Granfalloon to Karass

In Kurt Vonnegut's wonderful novel *Cat's Cradle*, he posits two tenets of his fabricated religion Bokononism: the granfalloon and the karass. A karass is a group of people who, unknown to them, are somehow affiliated or linked specifically to fulfill some higher purpose or the will of God. A granfalloon is a false karass, a seeming team that is meaningless in terms of the way God gets things done; examples are "the Communist Party, the Daughters of the American Revolution, the General Electric Company, the International Order of Odd Fellows and any nation, any time, anywhere."

In a sense, the family you create in the Business is your karass, while the family you are born into is more of a granfalloon. The former—unless you are Drew Barrymore, Ben Stiller, or Mamie Gummer—are likely to be more useful and more important to your success.

My college roommate Bill Connet (who egg-beat me to death in Christopher Durang's film adaptation of *The Brothers Karamazov*— ITYMATL) put together a wonderful folk band called Granfalloon, but I suggest you put together not a granfalloon but a karass. You may already be part of a relevant granfalloon: aspiring actors or Actors' Equity. Those groups are too large and too nonspecific to be of much use to you—though as a former president of Actors' Equity I can assure you that they do many wonderful things for their members.

Find your karass, your career karass. (Kareer karass?) You probably already have some members: the first adult who took your ambitions seriously, the teacher who encouraged you, the first director who cast you, the friend who thinks you're fantastically talented—even when you don't. Your true karass-building, however, will begin when you leave home, leave school, and set out to make your fortune, which begins with making your family.

Building a Family

If you are honest with yourself—or at least if you are like me—one of the reasons you decided to become an actor was the feeling of closeness, community, and camaraderie you experience in rehearsing and putting on a show. For that window of time, the rest of the company becomes your family.

In comparison, your own family—your family of origin as the social sciences describe it—may seem much less nurturing and accepting. Your family of origin is around you all the time, making demands on you (darn chores!), reminding you of the time they broke your favorite toy (darn little brother!), or the time they wouldn't let you go to that cool concert (darn dad!), or the time they made you wear that stupid outfit (darn mom!). Your love for your family is streaked with years of grudges and hurt and resentments, with the contempt or at least the taking-for-granted that familiarity breeds.

By contrast, your show family is a glittering bauble of irresistible novelty full of funny, charming, attractive, articulate people who like the same things you do. You bond with them. You share personal histories, perhaps a dressing room; you share the hopes, joys, and disasters of your production. You become incredibly close. You may fall in love with one of them. And then the show ends.

And then, if you're a professional actor, in a few weeks, months, or perhaps merely days, you get a new show family, and the process starts again. You may stay in touch with some of your former show family through social media or email. They may drop completely out of your life. You may think "What did I ever see there?" about the guy/gal you fell in love with. The whole experience may seem like a fever dream. One or more of the old show family may turn up in the new show family. (One of the silver linings to the challenging storm cloud of becoming a successful actor is that the number of people who work regularly is small—I often refer to Broadway as a village—and you will frequently work with folks you have worked with before and with people with whom you share a dozen mutual friends.)

Sometimes one or more of the people in your show family becomes part of your family of choice, your karass. You make the extra effort to stay in touch, to get together. You listen to their trouble and exult in their successes. You go see their shows. You support them and they support you; they are part of your support network. They help you cope with the difficulties of the Business. They commiserate with you and celebrate with you. In a business that offers a steady diet of no and rejection, these are the people who offer support and appreciation. They are an essential counterbalance to the

inevitable parade of disappointment, frustration, and missed opportunity—
and lack of opportunity.

Lack of opportunity is something to be addressed by the other group
you will spend your career accumulating: your team. If you family of choice
is there to buck you up when opportunity seems scarce or when you fail at
an opportunity you do get, your team is there to help increase the number of
your opportunities.

Your Team. Your Network (Network, Network)

Your team is the most useful, reliable, and count-on-able of your collection of
connection cards. As you climb your personal career mountain and become
more successful, you will add new members to your team, and some will drop
off. Your high school drama teacher and your mother's friend who did a bus
and truck of *Grease* will take a back seat to the dance teacher in your jazz class
and your accompanist who frequently plays for Broadway auditions.

Some of your friends in your family of choice may also be on your team,
and a team member can become a friend and part of your family of choice.
Generally, your family of choice supports you personally and you team supports you professionally. In a coldhearted transactional view of relationships,
you support and cheer your family of choice just as they support and cheer
you. It's a two-way street. If you have the right team, the support and assistance go one way. You are unlikely to be as useful to them as they are to you.

Your team is not an extension of you. It is not necessarily aligned with
your goals. It may not even particularly care about your career or your goals.
Yes, your agent or manager, when you get one, will be aligned with your goals,
but not exactly so. When your agent gets a breakdown (a list of the roles a
casting director is looking to cast), they may well submit two or more actors
on their roster of clients for each role. If they submit three actors including

you for a particular role and the casting director agrees to see the other two but not you, any tears your agent weeps are likely to be crocodile tears.

Crocodile tears or not, your agent will get 10 percent of your salary and a manager gets even more, so they have a financial interest in your success and your career. Other members of your team—casting directors, producers, composers, directors, authors, musical directors, choreographers, theatre owners, critics, journalists, veteran actors—have no financial stake in your success, so you need some other way of compensating them for being on your team.

This is where your graciousness, gratitude, and charm kick in. You thank these people. You show your appreciation. You praise and champion their work. You acknowledge their contribution to your life. You let them know how much their efforts mean to you. You thank them. You thank them again.

5
Outfitting Yourself: The Tools of the Trade

Before you set off to work or to look for work on the daunting slopes of Rejection Mountain, you will need your metaphorical carabiners, ice axe, harness, and belaying device: a headshot and résumé and audition material. These are your tools of the trade. These are the tools you will use to convince those who know you only slightly or not at all to see you and, once they see you, to hire you.

Headshots

Headshots, which can be a shot of just your head (face) or a bust view (head and shoulders) or three-quarter length (from the top of your head past your hips), have gone through many changes in style and popularity in my forty-plus years. Bordered. Unbordered. Portrait. Landscape. Indoor. Outdoor. Black and white. Color. Check with folks you know in the Business to find out what the flavor of the moment is. Head only? Three-quarters? Indoor? Outdoor? Portrait? Landscape? Border? No border? Name on front? No name?

You can make a case that I am the last person on Earth who should be advising anyone on headshots, because I just recently switched to what is, in essence, my third headshot in 40 years. That's pretty crazy—and not an example I would advocate anyone to follow. I had other headshots taken over the years and even duplicated several of them; I stuck with the winners. I'll give you the whole sordid history of the Wyman physiognomy and explain my rationale for sticking with the ones I did.

Wyman Through the Years

I can't believe I finally threw out the last copy of my first headshot, because it was a sure-fire laugh. As I referenced in "A Cautionary Tale," I was perhaps 23 with blond bangs and a wispy mustache. I wore a black turtleneck (the universal symbol for serious actor) in half the shots and a yellow Shetland pullover sweater with no shirt in the others. This double-edged stroke of genius left me the choice of a head floating in space against the black background or a pencil-necked fashion victim. The photographer's name was Joe something. I don't remember if someone referred me to him or if I found him in *Backstage* or what, but I do remember he was inexpensive: significantly less than $100. I don't blame Joe. I blame Nick for not doing a better job of investigating what a headshot should look like.

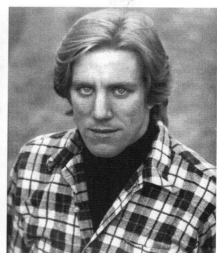

This disembodied head is a little casual.   A serious lumberjack. Seriously?

Shortly after my first Equity job, I had one of my castmates, Cliff Lipson, take some headshots of me. Cliff had photography skills and a very attractive price point: $0.00. We took some outdoor shots, and while the focus left a little something to be desired, they were a vast improvement over the floating-wispy-mustache head. (You'll notice I was still working the black turtleneck, but the plaid shirt and the coat took a bit of the curse off.) Twenty-first century Nick would like to tell young Nick to stop letting his hair flop over most of his forehead (this will be a recurrent problem in photo shoots to come). Invest in a little hair spray for Pete's sake.

Sometime later, Cliff took some more shots of me, indoors as well as out. I had grown a substantial mustache, which I shaved off halfway through the photo session (transitioning from the bartender in *Cowboy* back to the bossy husband in *Very Good Eddie*), and I had gotten rid of the black turtleneck.

My first believable headshot.   Ready to play cowboy heroes.

These two shots strike me as my first professional-looking headshots. The hair is very much of the '70s, and I seem to have something against buttoning down my collars, but the lad looks vaguely employable. Cliff Lipson, by the by, had already appeared on Broadway in *Hair* and *Jesus Christ Superstar* when I met him in my first Equity job. We went on to share a stage in the Broadway company of *The Magic Show* (for whose Broadway Show League softball team he played left field and I played first base for many years.). Despite his impressive career onstage, Cliff eventually turned to photography full time and is now one of the staff photographers for CBS Television. Sometimes even when the trail is smooth, you switch mountaintops. ITYMATL. In addition to sharing a softball field and a couple of cast lists, Cliff introduced me to his acting teacher Wynn Handman and has been a generous contributor over the years to the Wyman School of Poker Instruction. He is one of my favorite people on the planet.

In 1979, I used my television commercial earnings to hire a professional photographer. Richard Sutor, who had a huge Upper West Side apartment on 92nd Street, did a session with me that provided me with a headshot that I used for close to 15 years. Warning: do not follow this example and go 15 years between headshots.

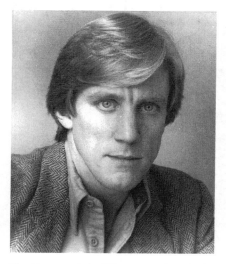

Nice blue eyes, but a little vague and uncertain.

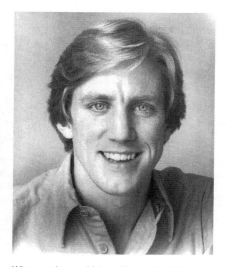

Winner, winner, chicken dinner. Used this shot for almost 20 years.

These are both nice shots, but the one on the right is the 15-year winner. It probably helped get me dozens of commercials. The guys on the left looks soulful and perhaps a little uneasily expectant—not really what Nick Wyman is selling.

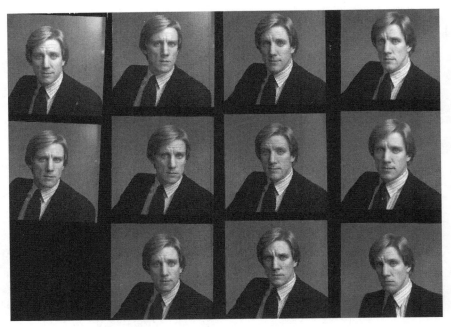

Unsuccessful young Republican candidate.

The other options—a) jacket and tie, and b) plaid sport shirt—did not seem like particularly viable options. Although I have definitely *become* a jacket-and-tie guy in my work, I wasn't so much in my late 20s, early 30s. And my hair is coiffed like a wig, giving me the look of some sleazy doofus of a local politician. The plaid shirt I think is a bit too much of a distraction: the visual equivalent of trying too hard.

Plaid shirt!! Way too distracting.

Straightforward, friendly guy.   Former cowboy star now playing bad guys.

After I began to feel chagrined at seeking employment for mid-40s Nick with a photo of 29-year-old Nick, I solicited suggestions for photographers from my agents, and after investigating a few, I chose Tess Steinkolk. I had a very good session with her and came away with another headshot that lasted me for 15 years. (Seriously. Ignore my example. Don't do this.)

Another longtime winner: a man with secret knowledge.

Having moved fully into my Jerk-in-a-Suit phase, I found the bottom photo to be just what I needed: calm, cool, confident and with a bit of I-know-and-you-don't in the eyes. The smiley guy is a great commercial shot, but even the commercials I was doing were looking for a Jerk in a Suit. As for Cowboy Gigolo/Badly-Aging Porn Star, the less said the better.

Sharp-eyed observers will have noticed the transition from Nicholas to Nick, and you may have even noticed that the last photo is bordered. I might still be trying to get away with a 20-year-old photo if color had not become de rigueur for a headshot. I turned to one of my best friends: Chase Newhart, who had journeyed back East from a multi-decade career in Hollywood as a first AD to return to one of his first loves—photography.

Wyman discovers color photography.   Titan of Industry.

Both shots are good, I think. The wrinkles give a gravitas to the smiling shot, and the serious guy is clearly a no-nonsense leader of men. That's me. Except for the no-nonsense part. (I'm sort of partial to nonsense.)

Picking a Photographer, Picking a Look

Picking a photographer is as fraught with the plethora of possibilities and the fear of failure (alliteration courtesy of my seventh-grade English teacher Ms. Eleanor Davis) as picking a mate. Prices vary widely, from two figures to four. You don't need to spend thousands, and you likely want to avoid the guy who will do it for $35. Somewhere in the hundreds is probably right. Word of mouth is perhaps the best recommendation. Casting directors and agents are the best and most experienced/professional sources of recommendations. If you're just starting out, you won't have an agent and probably won't know any casting directors, so ask your friends. Ask any professional union actors that you know. Put it out there.

Once you have some recommendations, check out the photographer's website. Do you respond well to the photos? Are they professional looking: in focus, well lit, not too busy? Do they seem like bland shots out of some corporate annual report, or do the individual personae of the actors come through? If the photos seem weird: poorly lit, too stiff, too sexy, too something else—move on. Call up the leading contenders and see how you respond to the person who will be behind the camera. Do you enjoy talking to them? If the photographer seems weird or cold (too stiff) or starts hitting on you (too sexy)—move on.

You want to feel comfortable with the photographer so that while he or she is taking these all-important, expensive photographs, you can relax, have a good time, and be completely yourself. Completely yourself. The essential you—that's what you want a photo of. You want to look good, but not so good that you are unrecognizable as you. If an agent or casting director calls you in based on a gorgeous photo and you walk in looking very little like your headshot, you will have done yourself no earthly good.

In addition to looking good while looking the way you basically look, you want to be in the ballpark of your long suit with your outfit. Many other guys in my CEO category wear jackets and ties. College student? Young mid-western mom? Slacker? Stoner? Hipster? Whatever your type, one of your set-ups/outfits—and probably one of the photos you select—should suggest that.

Back in the day (cue the video montage of Model T's, bread lines, poodle skirts), actors seeking work in on-camera commercials would use a "compos-ite" photo that showed the actor in various moods and in four to six different professions: exasperated plumber, smiling doctor, leering construction work-er, puzzled professor, and so forth. "Hey, look at all the roles I can play! Boy, am I versatile!" was the intended message.

Thankfully, those days are gone, I think, though dressing the part is still very much part of auditioning for television commercials. Actors not infre-quently come to NY auditions and change into a rudimentary costume or suggestion of a costume that they have brought. In LA, not having to endure the stares of folks on the subway, actors drive to auditions in full costume as cowboys, Indians, plumbers, doctors, and so forth. H. L. Mencken said, "No one ever went broke underestimating the intelligence of the American public." The corollary is that no commercial actor ever went broke underes-timating the intelligence of those who cast TV commercials, particularly the clients. For commercial auditions, I dress not in a costume, but in something that evokes the character. I make it a small step for for the clients' imagina-tion, not a running broad jump. Similarly, don't work at cross purposes with your headshot: wear things that fit with what you are likely to play.

Other wardrobe notes for your session? Don't let your clothes upstage you: avoid crazy styles, wild prints, bizarre costumes—anything that draws attention from what you're trying to sell (which is you, not the outfit). As a general rule, stay away from white and black, and find colors that set off and complement your natural coloring. I would also avoid the overly sexy shot (shirtless photos for guys, acres of cleavage for women), as they can turn off the more prudish casting folk or get you called in for the wrong reason. If, however, your long suit/strong suit is your sex appeal, if what people cast you as is rent boy or sexy vamp, then you probably want at least one of your shots to give casting folk a taste of that. A word to the wise: a little restraint and good taste go a long way.

To smile or not to smile: Traditionally, what you wanted to emerge with from your photo session was basically two shots: one smiling and one not. The smiling shot was your "commercial" shot, which you would use for TV commercials, sitcoms, musicals, and so forth—lighter fare. The serious expression was your "legit" shot, which you would use for projects of a darker or more serious nature, whether film, TV, or straight theatre. I still think this is the way to go, but your commercial shot no longer needs to be a completely white-bread Procter & Gamble cipher: you can have some edge, some character. What trumps everything else is that the photo should *look like you* and *evoke who you are*. When I was in doubt as to which was the appropriate choice for my headshot or which headshot was the appropriate choice for an audition, I usually went with the smiling guy. Remember, directors are hiring somebody that they will be spending a chunk of time with—they'd probably rather spend it with the smiling guy. This—how pleasant you are to be with—is a key thing to remember about auditioning. ITYMATL.

Once you have had your photo session, you will pick the winning shot(s). Once it was an 8 x 10 "contact sheet" with 36 images per page, over which you would pore with a magnifying glass. Now it is a password-protected website page that you can magnify on your tablet, your computer, or even your phone. The good news is that you will probably have several, perhaps many good choices in both the serious and smiling shots. The bad news is, you guessed it, that you will probably have several, perhaps many good choices in both the serious and smiling shots. So how to decide? How to even narrow it down?

Get other people's opinions, preferably people in the Business, preferably people who have some experience and/or expertise. Agents, casting folk, directors are all excellent sources of useful opinions. Moms, not so much. Your mother is likely to fall prey to picking the one that makes you look the best—or look how she likes to think of you. Remember, a photo in which you look fabulous may not represent the essential you.

Stray hairs, spots, and so forth can be easily airbrushed/photoshopped out. What you want to look for is a shot that makes you look good, that represents you well, and that has something going on in the eyes. Your headshot needs to connect with the casting agent and the director, and you can't do that with dead eyes.

So, let's step back to the photographer's studio. You need to keep your eyes alive. So you can't be frozen in one position, just staring at the camera. Turn away, then turn back to the camera. Take a break; get up and shake out your arms and legs to get the blood moving. When the photographer is taking the photo, have something going on in your mind. Be thinking something specific: it will show in your eyes. (This is also one of the keys to screen acting: thinking about something specific before, during, and after your lines.) The photographer can use lighting to put an actual glint in your eye; it's your job to put a metaphorical one in there. Think mischievous thoughts. Think flirtatious thoughts. (If you have some chemistry with the photographer, that can only make your photos better. Just remember Uncle Nick's words about restraint and good taste.)

So, with the assistance of everybody and their uncle, you pick out the winning shots: one smiling and one serious, or whatever you decide. You order a digital copy of these shots that you can email to all interested (and many uninterested) parties. You will also, in order to have hard copies to physically distribute, want to get them reproduced, probably 100 8 x 10 copies of each.

There are a number of places that specialize in this; my current favorite in NYC is Reproductions at 70 West 40th Street. As I said before, headshot styles change like Paris fashions. You will have checked with casting folk, agents, and other actors as to whether borders are currently in or out, whether your name on the front of the headshot is *de rigueur* or *de trop*.

Having picked up 100 copies in the currently fashionable style, you now have one of your key tools of the trade.

"You're gonna need new pictures."

Two handy marketing tools are photo postcards and business cards. If you meet someone in a social situation, it is a bit much to attempt to pawn off an 8 x 10 headshot and résumé on that person—assuming you have your headshots on you. However, a business card with a postage-stamp-size likeness of you and your contact info is the perfect choice. Similarly, as a follow-up to a meeting with an agent, a 4 x 6 postcard of your headshot avoids duplicating the 8 x 10 you hope he or she still has, and also helps put a face to the name on the correspondence. The website vistaprint.com is an excellent source for business cards, and they also do postcards. You might also check out www.overnightprints.com.

You will be emailing interested (or semi-interested) parties the JPEG of your headshot, but in most instances where you hand someone one of your precious hard copies, you will have attached your résumé to the back of it. So, you'll need a résumé.

Résumés

An actor's résumé is not like a business résumé. It is not a curriculum vitae detailing the specific responsibilities each of your previous jobs entailed. It is designed to give someone who doesn't know you a sense of who you are and what you've done. It is primarily a list of the roles you have played and the relevant facts (venue/significant people associated with the production).

First of all, in all caps at the top of the page and in probably the largest font on the page—YOUR NAME. Centered under that are the unions you belong to—AEA, SAG-AFTRA, AGMA, AGVA, SDC, and so forth. (No unions? Don't put anything there.)

Flanking your name, rectified to the margin on each side, are your contact information on the left and your height and weight on the right. (Many folks regularly fudge their height and weight figures: 5'2" becomes 5'4", 142 lbs. becomes 128 lbs., 5'10.5" becomes 6', and so forth. I am not going to be sanctimonious and tell you to be brutally honest, but I would certainly urge you to stay within the bounds of reasonably accurate.). Right under the height and weight, I would put your vocal range. (Not sure what you are? Ask some musical friend to listen to you and give you his or her opinion.)

Then you list your credits, breaking them down by category. In LA, Film and Television are the first two categories. In NY, Broadway (or Stage) is usually the first category. You may be saying, "But I haven't done any film or television or Broadway." The list may seem worrisomely thin to you. Fret not. If you are just starting out, you are just starting out—no one expects you to have done a dozen Broadway shows and six feature films.

The bottom section is Training. If you graduated from college, list the college and the degree. If you went to a theatre school, list that. List the individuals you studied with under the separate categories of Scene Study (or Acting), Voice, and Dance. Acting may have several subcategories: Scene Study, Text Analysis, Shakespeare, and so forth. Dance will frequently be broken down into Ballet, Tap, Jazz, Hip Hop, Modern, Gymnastics, and so forth. Just as you do not list your age on your résumé, do not list the year you graduated or the years you studied.

Speaking of gymnastics, under Training, I would also list Special Skills if you have them. Juggling? Gymnastics? Unicycle? Ukulele? Fluent Arabic? Baton-twirling? My friend Sophie Hayden, with whom I did *Whoopee!* in 1979, was a championship baton twirler in high school. The year after *Whoopee!* closed, she was twirling a baton in the original cast of *Barnum*. Her special skill certainly helped land her that role.

When you are just starting out, your Training section may be as big as or bigger than your list of credits. That's okay. Do not pad your list of credits by making things up. If you claim a bogus credit in a genuine production, life's mischievous karma will inevitably have you auditioning for the person who actually directed that production. He or she will not be amused. Similarly, making up imaginary productions to fill out your résumé lacks integrity and will, at best, leave you anxious about being found out. Self-esteem is tough enough to maintain in the Business without the damage of trashing your own integrity.

"Impressive resume, Elena. I'm a little curious about this gap you have between playing opposite Olivier in *Othello* and replacing Patti LuPone in *Evita*."

If you are just out of acting school or college, your credits should include the roles you did in school productions, any roles you did in summer stock, and any roles you did recently in community theatre. You might include a role or two from high school, particularly if it was reasonably age appropriate.

The shoe-polish-in-the-hair roles are of limited use to a casting person in figuring out whether or not you are right for a role your own age. Jay O. Sanders half-jokingly used to refer to his performance in *Death of a Salesman* at SUNY Purchase as "the world's greatest 21-year-old Willy Loman," but I don't think the credit shed much light on the essential Jay. But even if it was Lear or Polonius, if you did the role in a full-fledged production at college/acting school, put it in your credits. The one bit of truth stretching I might sanction is to list a role on which you did significant work in scene study class. Otherwise, I heavily frown on the listing of "suitable roles," "typical roles," or other hypothetical constructs.

Your résumé serves two purposes. Primarily, it serves as a summary of your experience—how many shows you have done, where you have done them, and what sort of roles you have done. It tells the reader whether you have a lot of experience or are just beginning. It tells the reader whether you have any professional experience. It tells the reader whether you have done musicals or plays or both, comic roles or serious roles or both, leading roles or only supporting roles.

Secondarily, your résumé serves as a conversation piece. In the struggle to make a career in Show Business, an initial battle is merely to get noticed, and the lifelong battle is to be memorable, to stake your claim to a little chunk of real estate in the minds of those who might get you work. ITYMATL. You want things on your résumé that will pique the interest of a director or casting agent—something that catches their eye, makes them want to ask you a question. To that end, you want to make sure that your résumé includes the name of anyone you have studied with or been directed by or acted with who has a significant profile in the Business. This is a forum in which I would not only condone name dropping, I would highly encourage it.

If Nick Wyman came to your school and talked to your class about how to make a career in the theatre, list "Business of Acting—Nick Wyman" under Training. If Jason Robert Brown came to your school to teach a master class: "Musical Theatre—Jason Robert Brown." If Michael Berresse directed you as Fastrada in your student production: "*Pippin* (directed by Michael Berresse)—Fastrada." If Liz Larsen was the Guest Artist Mama Rose at your university: "*Gypsy* (starring Liz Larsen)—Tulsa." Anyone with whom you have worked or studied who has a name to conjure with, this is the place to conjure with them.

This is also the way in which "Special Skills" can be most useful. If your special skill is amusing, out of the ordinary, or just plain weird, all the better. Generally, you want your special skill to have some plausible relevance to potential stage or screen work—hence, gymnastics, playing the violin, fluent German. However, these skills will interest someone one in 10—no, maybe one in 100 times. Rodeo Clown, Hula Hoop Champion, Fire Eater may be useful to almost no one, but they will intrigue everyone and are likely to get the person auditioning you to say "Fire Eater?" That is golden. You will stick in their memory. You hope that your audition burns an indelible image of talent in their brain as well, but at least they will remember you—and that's something that won't be true for most of those auditioning.

Oh, one other thing about your résumé. If you are printing it on 8 1/2" x 11" paper, you will need to cut it down to fit neatly on the back of your 8 x 10 headshot. Consequently, you need to make sure that all your info fits on an 8 x 10 surface and that it will be centered when you trim the standard-sized paper. Attach the résumé to your headshot with a glue stick or three/four staples. There are services that will print your résumé on the back of your headshot. I find this a bit of a frozen-in-amber approach to one's career; I would prefer to project the image of someone who is constantly adding credits to his/her résumé. To that end, rather than printing a new résumé every time you get a job, I find it perfectly acceptable—perhaps even advisable—to write your latest credit in ink in the appropriate spot. Don't do this for more than two credits or it begins to look less like the résumé of a constantly-working actor and more like the résumé of a lazy, tightfisted actor.

```
NICHOLAS WYMAN                          Height: 6' 4"  Weight: 190 lbs.
32 Washington Square                    Hair: Blond    Eyes:  Blue
New York, N.Y.   10011                  Voice:  Baritone
(212) 228-7045 (home)
      541-7600 (service)

                         NEW YORK

Portfolio Studios
     Jones & Schmidt's "Philemon" (dir. by Tom Jones) - Servillus

Theatre St. Clements
     "Camino Real" (dir. by Estelle Parsons) - Kilroy

Manhattan Theatre Club
     "La Ronde" (dir. by Madeleine Sherwood) - the Count

Van Dam Theatre
     "The Butter and Egg Man" (dir. by Stephen Book) - McClure
     "Love's Labors Lost" (dir. by Mel Shapiro) - Berowne
     "Our Town" (dir. by Therese Hadyn) - Editor Webb

                    HARVARD UNIVERSITY
"Uncle Vanya" - Dr. Astrov
"Anthony and Cleopatra" - Ventidius
"The Zoo Story" - Jerry
"A Funny Thing. . ." - Miles Gloriosus
1972 Hasty Pudding Show - Mayor DeBluesaway
1971 Hasty Pudding Show - Squamish Carstairs
"Pirates of Penzance" - Pirate King
"Funny Girl" - Ziegfeld Tenor

                         STOCK

Metropolitan Musical Theatre          Crackersport Music Theatre
     "Celebration" - Potemkin              "Carnival!" - Paul
"Oliver" - Fagin                      "Zorba" - Zorba
"Roar of the Greasepaint..." - Sir    "1776" - Jefferson
"Pirates of Penzance" - Pirate King
"Peter Pan" - Captain Hook
"The Mikado" - Pooh-Bah                Overlook Musical Theater
"A Funny Thing. . ." - Senex               "Annie Get Your Gun"-Frank Butler

                         TRAINING

Circle-in-the-Square Theatre Workshop (1972-1974):
          Acting:  Nikos Psacharopoulos, David Margulies, Stephen Book
          Speech:  Joan Langue
          Dance:   Willa Kahn, Judy Blackstone
          Voice:   Gertrude Tingley
```

My first résumé—probably fall 1974—takes the prize both for the amount of effort/creativity that went into it and the amount of white space on the page. Only one lie (I did Zoo Story in high school, not at college), and I was smart enough to throw in every recognizable name I could. I list my address—something I don't recommend—and I list no unions (because I didn't belong to any). I draw your attention to my "service" phone number: yes, actors had answering services (answering services!) and one would make a 10-cent (10 cents!) call from a phone booth (phone booths!) to see if an agent had called.

NICHOLAS WYMAN
AEA - SAG - AFTRA

(212) 874-1716 machine

Ht.:   6'5"   Wt.:   200 lbs.
Hair: Blond   Eyes: Blue
Voice: Baritone

BROADWAY

"The Phantom of the Opera"	Monsieur Firmin
"The Musical Comedy Murders of 1940"	Patrick O'Reilly
"Doubles"	Chuck
"My Fair Lady"	Freddy Eynsford-Hill
"On the Twentieth Century"	Bruce Granit
"Whoopee!"	Sheriff Bob
"The Magic Show"	Feldman the Magnificent
"Very Good Eddie"	Percy Darling
"Grease"	Vince Fontaine

FILM

"Rude Awakening"	Dr. Albert
"Funny Farm"	Dirk Criterion
"Planes, Trains & Automobiles"	New York Lawyer
"Weeds"	Assoc. Warden Wilson

TELEVISION

"Travelin'" (pilot)	Larry Birch
"The Murder of Mary Phagan"	Lund
(NBC Miniseries)	
"Who's The Boss"	Dr. Carter
"Best of Families" (PBS Miniseries)	Johannson
"The Dain Curse" (CBS Miniseries)	Whitey

OFF BROADWAY

"Angry Housewives"	Larry Prince
"Once on a Summer's Day"	Charles Dodgson
"Kennedy at Colonus"	LBJ, Gov. Ross Barnett, J. Edgar Hoover, Ken, Joe Kennedy, Jr., Joseph Kennedy, Sr.
"When We Dead Awaken"	Ulfhejm
"Charlotte Sweet"	Bob Sweet
"Paris Lights"	F. Scott Fitzgerald, James Joyce

REGIONAL

Guthrie Theatre:	"Twelfth Night" - Orsino
Arena Stage:	"Beyond Therapy" - Bruce
O'Neill Theatre Center:	"Portrait of Jennie" - Arne
	"Shakespeare and the Indians" - Mace
Pittsburgh Public Theater:	"Of Mice and Men" - Lennie
Barter Theatre:	"Oh Coward"
	"The Apple Tree" - Adam, Sanjar, Flip
Hartford Stage Co.:	"Holiday" - Nick Potter

Fifteen years later, I'm taller (I think I shaved an inch off in my 1974 résumé) and heavier, and I have an answering machine. I have 10 Broadway credits and half a dozen credits in each of the other areas. I've stopped listing names; my credits are sufficient to start a conversation. The '80s were good to me.

NICK WYMAN

AEA • SAG • AFTRA

CONTACT:
HWA - 212-889-0800
PARADIGM (Commercials) - 212-246-1030

Ht.:   6'5"   Wt.: 215 lbs.
Hair: Blond   Eyes: Blue
Voice: Baritone

BROADWAY

"Les Miserables" (10th Anniv. Cast)	Thenardier
"The Phantom of the Opera"	Monsieur Firmin
"The Musical Comedy Murders of 1940"	Patrick O'Reilly
"Doubles"	Chuck
"My Fair Lady"	Freddy Eynsford-Hill
"On the Twentieth Century"	Bruce Granit
"Whoopee!"	Sheriff Bob
"The Magic Show"	Feldman the Magnificent
"Very Good Eddie"	Percy Darling
"Grease"	Vince Fontaine

FILM

"Igby Goes Down"	Suit
"Private Parts"	Douglas Kiker
"Die Hard With A Vengeance"	Targo
"Mr. Chief Justice"	John Marshall
"Rude Awakening"	Dr. Albert
"Funny Farm"	Dirk Criterion
"Planes, Trains & Automobiles"	New York Lawyer
"Weeds"	Assoc. Warden Wilson

TELEVISION

"Big Apple"	Parker
"Spin City"	Polluting CEO
"Law and Order"	Judge Mikkelson
"One Life To Live"	Peter Manning
"Pete and Pete"	Coach Nahrens
"Travelin'" (pilot)	Larry Birch
"The Murder of Mary Phagan" (NBC Miniseries)	Lund
"Who's The Boss"	Dr. Carter

OFF BROADWAY

"The Misanthrope"	Covington
"Three in the Back, Two in the Head"	Jackson
"Hunchback of Notre Dame"	Frollo
"Breaking Legs"	Terence O'Keefe
"Angry Housewives"	Larry Prince
"Kennedy at Colonus"	LBJ, Gov. Ross Barnett, J. Edgar Hoover, Ken, Joe Kennedy, Jr., Joseph Kennedy, Sr.
"When We Dead Awaken"	Ulfhejm

REGIONAL

Paper Mill Playhouse	"Applause" - Howard Benedict
	"Sweeney Todd" – Judge Turpin
Goodman Theatre	"Another Midsummer Night" - Oberon
Berkshire Theatre Festival	"Quartermaine'sTerms" - Henry Windscape
	"Brimstone" - Seamus
Williamstown Theatre Festival	"1776" - Jefferson
Guthrie Theatre	"Twelfth Night" - Orsino
Arena Stage:	"Beyond Therapy" - Bruce
Pittsburgh Public Theater	"Of Mice and Men" - Lennie
Barter Theatre	"Oh Coward"
	"The Apple Tree" - Adam, Sanjar, Flip
Hartford Stage Co	"Holiday" - Nick Potter
	"Loot" - Truscott

Another 12 or 13 years brings us to 2002, and despite my dropping a number of credits off my résumé, the print is smaller and the 8 x 10 space is jammed. I list my agents now, not my home number. Oh, and I keep getting heavier.

NICK WYMAN
AEA SAG-AFTRA

Contact:

Ht.: 6'4" Wt.: 220
Hair: Blond Eyes: Blue
Voice: Baritone

BROADWAY:

Network	Arthur Jensen
Catch Me If You Can	Roger Strong
Tale of Two Cities	John Barsad
Sly Fox	Captain Crouch
Les Miserables	Thenardier
Musical Comedy Murders of 1940	Patrick O'Reilly
Doubles	Chuck
My Fair Lady	Freddy Eynsford-Hill
On the Twentieth Century	Bruce Granit
Very Good Eddie	Percy Darling

FILM: *Undiscovered Country* — *Vincent*

Synecdoche, NY	Soap Actor Doctor
Maid in Manhattan	Concierge
Igby Goes Down	Undertaker
Die Hard with a Vengeance	Targo
Mr. Chief Justice	John Marshall
Funny Farm	Dirk Criterion
Planes, Trains and Automobiles	New York Lawyer

TELEVISION:

"Elementary"	Duncan Brice
"VEEP"	Quincy Carter
"Boardwalk Empire"	Dr. Landau
"One Life to Live"	Peter Manning
"The Murder of Mary Phagan"	Lund

OFF-BROADWAY:

Desperate Measures	Governor
The Fartiste	Aristide Bruant
The Misanthrope	Covington
Breaking Legs	Terence O'Keefe

REGIONAL:

Asolo Repertory Theatre	All the Way – LBJ
Long Wharf Theatre	The Second Mrs. Wilson - Cabot
Guthrie Theatre	Twelfth Night – Orsino
Arena Stage	Beyond Therapy – Bruce
Hartford Stage	Age of Innocence – Hickey, etc.
	Loot – Truscott
	Holiday – Nick Potter
Goodman Theatre	Another Midsummer Night – Oberon
Berkshire Theatre Festival	Quartermaine's Terms – Windscape
Pittsburgh Public Theatre	Of Mice and Men – Lennie

This is my current résumé. I continue to cull credits from the list, and I continue to gain weight. (I actually got up to 235 a couple years ago; I'm now back below 220.) Gravity has gained the upper hand in the height department: I'm back down to 6'4". Notice the hand-inked addition to my credits.

The Union(s)

To join or not to join. In the past, joining the union was the goal of every aspiring actor. A few actors today, when presented with the opportunity, delay or even abjure joining Equity or SAG-AFTRA. They are getting work—either in non-Equity tours or in non-SAG commercials—and they are making some money. They fear that if they join the union, the competition will be much more intense, and they will lose all those non-union "opportunities."

I put "opportunities" in quotes because non-union work is the opportunity to work for less compensation and with fewer protections. On a non-Equity tour, actors may make what seems like a decent salary; but they will earn no retirement benefits, their per diem will not cover three decent meals, they are unlikely to receive health coverage, they may well be forced to double up in their hotel room, and there are no mandatory rest periods and no limitations on travel time. On a non-SAG commercial, you will get a one-time fee (instead of a stream of residual payments), you will get no health coverage or retirement benefits, you may have given away forever your right to do a commercial for a conflicting product, and that filmed image may remain forever the property of the advertiser (so heaven help you if an embarrassing spot resurfaces when you finally get considered for a TV pilot).

Non-union work can give you experience and enable you to hone your skills. But as soon as you feel you have sufficient experience and expertise, you should absolutely join the union(s) at your earliest opportunity. That is how you will protect your present and your future. There are many in the union who feel that a non-union actor is not a professional actor, that the only professional actors are union actors. To those who would quibble with this and say that it is the salary that makes an actor a professional, that any paid actor is a professional actor, to them I say that while non-union actors may be paid (and some of them fairly well), the only career actors are union actors. If you are in this business for the long haul, you want to be hauling around a union card. Here is what I wrote about the subject as the president of one such union:

"To Join or Not to Join? My Rejoinder"

At our January Eastern membership meeting, a member asked what to say to young nonmembers who are trying to figure out whether they should join Actors' Equity as soon as possible or wait a while or just keep working non-Equity. In response, a couple of members gave heart-warming testimonials on the value of AEA. We have no official AEA party line, but let me weigh in with my personal response.

Surprisingly, your president does not adjure every young actor to grab his or her Equity card at the first opportunity. My advice is to wait until you're ready: get your training, get experience. Develop those chops, build that résumé. Then, when you are ready to compete with the very best, go for it—and go for it full out, as Jerry Mitchell says. And don't hesitate overlong before jumping in: the lookism and physical demands of the Business can make one's 20s some of one's most employable years.

Another argument for sooner rather than later is that a union card offers one the opportunity through Equity Principal Auditions and Equity Chorus Calls to be seen for desirable jobs. A young Michigan grad told me how grateful she was that after a stint at the St. Louis MUNY, she had taken the opportunity to get her Equity card. Because of EPAs and ECCs, she was getting in on auditions for Broadway and touring and LORT jobs for which her classmates, who hadn't had or hadn't availed themselves of the same opportunity, were unable to be seen.

I have heard of people making the argument that they plan to stay non-Equity because if they "go Equity" they will never work or work much less. This line of reasoning is fear based, and anybody who thinks that way is unlikely to make a career of the theatre. And I very strongly feel that anyone who wants to make a career of the Theatre *has* to be Equity. Why would one not want the opportunity to work at the very highest level of the Business? Why would on not want the protection and support of bargained-for working conditions? Why would one not want a defined benefit pension?

And for those who claim they don't need a union because their non-Equity job pays them good money, I say that a non-Equity job that pays good money is an Equity job in waiting. We are committed to organizing, to creating more work opportunities for the members, and we will move aggressively to bring any theatrical employer with the ability to pay decent salaries into the Equity fold.

And perhaps most importantly, union is solidarity. Our union is 50,000 people supporting one another in a very difficult business, 50,000 people committed to creating the best opportunities for one another to make a life in the theatre. Why on earth would an actor or stage manager wish to give their energy and talents to an enterprise that vitiated, undermined, or militated against the success and efforts of their fellow workers? Theatre is family. Union is family. Why would one hurt one's family members?

So, what I say to young people considering whether or when to go Equity is this: if you are determined to have a career in the theatre, you *need* to be Equity. First get your training and get some experience, but do it as quickly as you can; and as soon as you feel ready to compete with the pros, do whatever you can to *get that card*! I will be proud to sign it.

Where to Find Work Opportunities

Back in the day—and that day was the 1920s, 1930s, 1940s, and 1950s—an actor looked for work by going around to the offices of the various Broadway producers and asking if they had any potential work, any shows about to be cast. "No, nothing today" was the usual response. The actor would repeat this on a regular basis until he or she got work or got sick of looking for work. As you can imagine, it was very time intensive. It was also very shoe-leather intensive, which is why Conrad Cantzen in his will provided a fund for Actors' Equity members to be able to get a new pair of shoes every year. (Shoes are more expensive now, and the Conrad Cantzen Fund now provides $50 toward a pair of shoes every other year.)

An actor could also read *Variety*—a weekly journal of all things Show Business that comes out on Wednesdays—to see what projects might be brewing. In 1941 Leo Shull started mimeographing a four-page daily listing of casting information; this evolved into a weekly tabloid called *Show Business*. In 1960 *Show Business* employees Allen Zwerdling and Ira Eaker left to start *Backstage*, a rival weekly tabloid. By the early 1970s when I happened along, *Backstage* and *Show Business* had established themselves as *the* source of information for aspiring and early-career actors. The papers came out on Thursday, so it was not unusual for actors to get up early on Thursday, dress themselves in all-purpose nice audition clothes, and invest a quarter at the local newsstand for *Backstage* or *Show Business* sometime between 8:00 and 9:00 a.m. Opening the paper, one would quickly scan the listings for any suitable auditions being held that same day. If there were one (or more), off you would go to sign up for the chance to be seen and heard for the job(s).

In today's Internet age, *Backstage*, which has a companion *Backstage West*, is still hanging on as a weekly publication (and one with many useful articles as well as their casting notices); and its website, www.backstage.com, lists auditions all across the country. They are a good—perhaps the leading—source of information about non-union jobs and such low-pay/no-pay opportunities as showcases and student films. Actors' Equity jobs are also listed in *Backstage*, and you can subscribe to daily email casting information at www.broadway-world.com/casting. (Equity members will find casting notices updated daily in the "Casting Call" section of the Equity website's member portal.) You need to be an Equity member to ensure your being seen at these auditions, but many of the auditions allow for the possibility of non-Equity actors being seen as time permits. In practicality, what that means is arriving early and frequently waiting hours in a holding area for a gap (that may or may not materialize) in the scheduled Equity auditions.

In addition to the required Actors' Equity auditions, employers sometimes hold "open calls" (auditions for union and non-union talent) for their shows. This is particularly true of shows that require young cast members (*Les Miz, Grease, Matilda, Annie, Spring Awakening, Bring It On*) or that require unusual skills or characteristics (Deaf West's revival of *Spring Awakening*, *Barnum*, the recent revival of *Pippin*). You don't need an agent or a union card for these auditions, and they are a great opportunity not only to be seen by directors, choreographers, musical directors, and casting people but possibly to get a job.

There are other ways to get seen for a currently running show—or at least move yourself to the top of the pile of possible replacements. You can reach out directly to the director (or choreographer or musical director) by writing them c/o the theatre. Once again, a clever, charming note (don't forget to praise their work!) will help ensure that your picture and résumé are not "round filed." Perhaps an even better route is to write a note to the production stage manager. He or she will probably have little say in the casting of the show's replacements, but will definitely have the ear of the director when it comes to recommending possible people to see.

Formerly called *Ross Reports*, a Show Business classic that maintains its relevance is *Call Sheet*, published twice a year by Samuel French ($20). This is a booklet listing contact information for agents, casting directors, and television series in both NY and LA. This will tell you who works at various talent agencies and casting offices. It will tell you where a TV show is shot and who casts it. It will give you phone numbers and addresses. It's a great resource. Sue Porter Henderson publishes *Henderson's Casting Directors Guide* twice a year; it is $14 for the hard copy, $10 for the PDF download.

The fullest compendium of information on upcoming shows is *Theatrical Index*, which comes out weekly. You can subscribe to the online version for $19.95 per month, or you can sample a single hard copy for something less than that. *American Theatre* magazine, published by Theatre Communications Group ($40 annual membership), lists the plays being done and about to be done at theatres across the country. Other resources for information about prospective shows and stage projects are the websites playbill.com, broadway.com, and broadwayworld.com. These websites provide legitimate information about shows in the planning and casting stages and can give you some idea of jobs you might target. Another, somewhat less legitimate, Internet source of information about what is happening in the biz and what is on the horizon are the chat rooms allthatchat.com, the chat room on broadway-world.com, and so forth.

These interactive threads are populated by some Broadway insiders, some folks with a profile in the industry, and a lot of fangirls, fanboys, and theatre geeks. These sites are full of lots of passion for the theatre and about specific shows, both the popular and the unpopular—which is a wonderful thing. They are also full of gossip and snark, some of it very mean-spirited—which is not at all a wonderful thing. As you sift and sort and surf through the breathless observations/revelations and the frequently catty opinions, you may well discover some worthwhile news about shows in the planning stages and roles being vacated by departing performers. If you yourself begin posting on these sites, I urge you to bear in the mind the words of Deborah Kerr in *Tea and Sympathy*: "When you speak of this . . . be kind."

6
Beginning the Climb

Looking for Work

Auditions

Auditions are what you do as an actor. They are an essential part of the Business for all but the very, very tippy-top of the pyramid, the 1/100th of one percent, the Meryl Streeps and Tom Hankses who simply get offered roles. Indeed, my attitude is that my real work as an actor is not the rehearsing and performing for money—that's sort of the reward (at least for the first few months of the job—ITYMATL). The real work is *looking* for work: keeping my skills sharp; scouting out possible jobs; networking; making connections and staying connected; urging agents, casting folk, and directors to see me; preparing for auditions—and the auditions themselves. This work—the looking for work—occupies the majority of my time, sometimes even during those weeks when I am actually being paid to act.

So, if this is the work, if this is what you are going to be doing for a living, if this is how you will probably spend the majority of your time, you want it to be satisfying, fulfilling, enjoyable, and productive. Let's assume you have succeeded in the first part of your task: you have gotten an audition. Now what?

There are two types of auditions: auditions for a specific role in a specific project and an interview/go-see/general audition. Let's focus on the latter. A general audition is typical of your first encounter with a prospective agent. Some casting offices hold general auditions to get to know new talent. A general audition is necessary to get into the acting or musical theatre programs of most of the better universities and conservatories. Also, some theatres—notably LORT theatres with a variety of shows in their season—have general auditions.

A general audition is BYO. Instead of having to eat whatever the host has prepared, you get to plan, prepare, and share a delicious feast. So, what should be on the menu?

Your bread and butter, to overload (overlard?) the metaphor, should consist of two monologues and two songs. One song will be a ballad, one song will be an up-tempo number. One monologue will be comic, one will be more serious. Additionally, one monologue might be contemporary and one might be classical. Your repertoire of both monologues and songs will grow, but these are the basics.

Monologues

Although you will use your audition songs again and again over the years when you audition for specific roles (even when the creative team also ask you to learn one of the character's songs), your monologues have a much more limited usefulness. However, your monologues are your live-action calling card; they are frequently your introduction to acting teachers, agents, and casting people. You want that material to represent you well.

The libraries and bookstore have many collections of monologues. You can find suggestions online. I would suggest two components of a successful monologue: 1) it should be reflective of your age and type, and 2) it should be material that speaks to you, that energizes you, that you relate to. You might be able to fudge the first; the second is inviolate.

What is the purpose of your monologue? It is to show off your abilities (Hey, look at me, I can *act*!); but more particularly, it is to reveal who you are, something of the essential you. So although it would be disconcerting to the auditor for you to do a monologue that famously and clearly was written for someone of the opposite gender and/or forty years older, that might well take second place to your feelings for the material and how strongly you feel it conveys the essential you, what you have to sell.

"They loved your monologue, honey, so when you're done here,
they want to hear a funny song."

If you are looking for a Shakespeare monologue, try www.shake-speare-monologues.org. Although there are Shakespearean monologues that speak to me personally, that resonate deeply with me, I believe a contemporary monologue is a more useful calling card. (Shakespeare's not writing much anymore: *CSI: Stratford* was a flop, and the studios aren't returning his calls.) Although doing a Shakespeare or Shaw monologue can demonstrate your ability with language, it is all but impossible to make a living doing Shakespeare and Shaw.

If, as you look for contemporary monologues that speak to you, you are anxious about engendering an eye-rolling, not-this-again reaction from your auditor, consider two less recherché sources: movie scripts and your own mind. Film is a visual medium; it's not about soliloquizing actors or even talking heads, so scenes in which one actor does all the talking for a minute or more are fairly uncommon, but there are some. (In the script of *Die Hard with a Vengeance,* Jeremy Irons's character had a long, bravura speech about what made gold special, what separated it from all other objects of thievery. Jeremy, who had been to the rodeo before, explained to me that filmmakers lured stars into making movies by giving their characters fabulous soliloquies, and once filming was completed, the soliloquies ended up on the cutting-room floor. A decent chunk of Jeremy's gold rant, though, ended up in the movie.) A fool-proof route to novelty is to write your own monologue. This is not for the faint of heart, because it compounds the challenge of acting well not only with the challenge of writing well, but the challenge of writing an interesting, compelling, emotionally resonant one-minute scene well.

Some monologues are done to death. (Karen Kohlhass lists overdone monologues at www.monologueaudition.com.) Even if you are doing an old chestnut that the auditor has heard a dozen times before, you can still give a winning performance. The key is to make it fresh and true and specific. There are undoubtedly dozens and dozens of ways to approach an acting text, and I promised in the intro that this would not be a book on how to act, but let me make a few basic suggestions.

Acting in the Audition

Newspaper reporters are told to answer the basic *W* questions: Who? What? Where? When? Why? Actors should basically ask themselves the same questions.

WHO? Who am I? Who am I speaking to?

WHAT? What is our relationship? What do I feel about the other person? What just happened before I start talking? What happens in the scene/ monologue? What do I learn?

WHERE? Where am I? Is this place comfortable? Dangerous?

WHEN? When does this take place—in the day, in the year, in my life? When in my relationship with the other person does it take place?

WHY? Why am I talking? Why do I choose to say each thing I say? What do I hope to achieve? What problem am I trying to solve?

Unless you are performing material from the role you are auditioning for, in which case your answers should at least conform to the given circumstances of the scene and the character, the answers don't have to be "right." They just need to be clear and specific and preferably strong.

Make bold choices. Making bold choices is like the old sport cliché: playing to win instead of playing not to lose. If a director is seeing twelve people for a role (and the director might well be seeing many, many more than that), you have to know that ten of those twelve are going to be believable and make sense of the words. If you are going to get the job, you have to do something more. (And by something more, I don't mean ripping off your top, slapping your scene partner, or sweeping the director's lunch off the table.)

You can try intensifying your current choices. Instead of liking the person you're talking to, love them, be crazy about them; instead of disliking them, loathe them. But be specific. Maybe you love the person's elbows and you keep trying to sneak peeks at them. Maybe you love the way they say the word "evening" and you shiver every time they say it. Maybe the other person is the monster who killed your parents, and you are studying them for the moment you can strike them in their most vulnerable spot. The choices, as I said, don't have to be in the script. To be clear about clarity, the choices need to be clearly made and clear to you; they don't have to be clear to your auditor. Secrets can be empowering.

A word about choices. The casting director Andy Roth says there are three bad choices and three good choices. The bad choices: 1) not making a choice, 2) not committing to your choice, and 3) choosing something clearly contradicted by the material and the given circumstances. The three good ones: 1) the exact choice the casting director had in mind, 2) a different choice but one the casting director likes as much or more than his/her own, and 3) a strong, clear wrong choice that lets the casting director say, "Thanks. Now try it this way."

While your choices don't necessarily have to gibe with what's in the script, what's in the script has to be in your performance. Study the text for clues like a Talmudic scholar, like an archaeologist, like one of those forensic geeks on a TV procedural. What happens in the scene? Find the event(s). Note every new bit of information. Note every change of direction, every change of intention, and within every intention, every change in the mode of approach/attack.

If your monologue or scene is a comic one, these changes of direction are key to the comedy. Frequently the "funny" lies in a character strongly heading

in one particular direction and then sharply redirecting herself (or being forcibly redirected) or suddenly slamming to a stop. The clearer, cleaner, and sharper those directions and movements are, the funnier the scene will be.

If you have been provided with material from the show you are auditioning for—sides or suggested scenes—prepare the hell out of those scenes. Study them. Study them some more. Ask yourself those *W* questions. Know the lines backwards and forwards. For a stage production, you don't strictly need to memorize the lines and you will be holding the script/sides in your hand, but you want to be in the scene with your auditioning partner, not buried in the script.

Audition Songs

Everything I said about performing a monologue or a scene applies equally to performing a song. You need to know who you're talking (singing) to, why you are saying (singing) this, where you are, what just happened, what you hope to achieve, and so forth. It is a little scene. You have to act; you can't just make beautiful sounds. A disconcertingly large percentage of people auditioning can make beautiful sounds. You will need to make sounds—beautiful or not—with a purpose. Where once musicals employed an ensemble of singers and an ensemble of dancers as well as actors to play the small roles,

now they employ an ensemble of singer-dancers (or dancer-singers) who have to act well enough to play those small roles.

That's the bad news about what has changed in sixty years. The good news is that, as I said before, you no longer need to sing like John Raitt or Ethel Merman. Of course, it doesn't hurt if you do. However, everyone these days is amplified, so even if your voice could never fill a hall on its own, despair not. If you can act and you can carry a tune, you've got a shot at musicals.

You will need at least two songs: a ballad and an up-tempo. The ballad will show off more of your voice—its quality and its range; it will also probably show off your acting more, your ability to tell a story. Your up-tempo will be more about rhythm and personality, how you move, how you "sell" a song. Of the two, the ballad is the more important tool for selling yourself.

In picking your audition song, you want something that shows you off well. Most particularly, it needs to fit your vocal range. If you can hit the final note of the song as long as you've gotten ten hours sleep and the pollen count has been zero for three days running, that is not the song for you. Stay within yourself. I can sing A-flats and the occasional A, but the money note in my go-to audition song is an F. There was this one time, however, when I tried to sing a high B natural. . . .

It is 1986, and they are casting the original Broadway company of *Les Misérables*. I love the story and the music. My agents think I'm right for Javert, but Trevor Nunn has decided to go with his *Cats* actor Terry Mann. That's okay with me, because I want to play Jean Valjean: I love that role. Those auditioning have to prepare "Bring Him Home" and "Who Am I," so I buy the London recording and start practicing. My wife and I go up to the country for the day to visit Mandy Patinkin and his wife. (Mandy and my wife were classmates and buddies at Juilliard, our first-born children are the same age, and they lived in the building behind ours in NYC.) Mandy is busy practicing swordplay (he's about to go off to do *The Princess Bride*), and

I'm busy singing Boublil and Schoenberg. Mandy says to me, "Oh yeah, they talked to me about playing Valjean, but the real role is Thenardier."

Sadly, I don't listen to Mandy, and I keep working on Valjean. Comes the day of the audition. I go down to 890 Broadway, and I sing "Bring Him Home." At least, I think I sang "Bring Him Home," but maybe I never got to it. All I remember is that I did sing "Who Am I." As I approached the end of the song, a combination of adrenalin, chutzpah, and stupidity told me not to flip up into a head voice falsetto for the high B natural on the "one" of "2-4-6-0-1!" but instead to sing it full voice. I believe there is still an ugly stain on the walls of 890 Broadway from my hideous last note.

So don't sing notes you can't sing. Don't sing notes you can occasionally sing. Sing what you *know* you can sing. If you have glorious high notes (or low notes), by all means sing them—just don't sing the notes at the furthest reaches of your range.

Choosing your audition song is much like choosing an audition monologue: it needs to speak to you, to resonate with you. It should give you something to act, a story to tell. Your voice teacher or accompanist or musical director may have suggestions. Your friends may have ideas, but remember that what floats their boat may do nothing for you.

Also be aware that some songs become overused and you will have little chance to overcome the musical director's despair if this is the tenth time that day he has heard "Meadowlark" or whatever. When I was starting out, every guy was singing "Corner of the Sky" from *Pippin*. Fifteen years later, every other guy was singing "Anthem" from *Chess*. Choosing the road less traveled by will make all the difference.

You may be asked to sing a rock song or a country-western song or a comic song or a pop song or a tragical-comical-historical-pastoral song. If you have musical skills and/or you are a quick study, work them up. Most people who do musical comedy build and create a "book:" a loose-leaf binder of ten to a couple dozen songs that they are ready to sing at the drop of a five-minute audition slot. Then, when the musical director asks if you have something that shows off your high belt or your sense of humor or simply "something else," you will have things to suggest.

If your musical skills are rudimentary or so marginal that it was all you could do to learn that one ballad and that one up-tempo, fear not. Go in and sing your ballad. If they ask you for a rock song or a country-western song or whatever, tell them you don't have one of those with you but that you will gladly learn one of the songs from their show if they wish. Of course, if they accede to your offer (calling your bluff, as it were) then you have to learn the song.

Actors are not infrequently these days asked to learn a song or two from a new work. It makes a certain sense: the creators can compare apples to apples as each auditioning actor sings the same song—the song that character needs to sing in the show. It favors those who are a quick study and does a disservice to those who may do brilliant work with a piece of material but who take a while to get there.

Whether you are a quick study or not, you want to prepare the hell out of any new work excerpt you are given to audition. The casting folks will generally send you the sheet music and frequently an MP3 of the song, either with just the accompaniment or with someone doing the vocal. If you are musically gifted, this is all you need to work on the song. If, like me, you have the musical gifts of your average cow, you will need some help. Get an accompanist or musical director to work on the song with you. If you can't do it in person, you can use the app Harmony Helper (harmonyhelper.com) as a do-it-yourself practice aid, or you can send the music off to an accompanist friend who will record it for you. It helps me to make a recording of just _my_ notes—the notes of my melody without any accompaniment. I also like to have, if casting hasn't supplied it, a recording of someone singing my part/my song along with the accompaniment as well as a recording of just the accompaniment. Then practice, practice, practice.

If you are singing their song from their show, it makes sense to use their accompanist, the person they have hired to play the piano for those auditioning. If you are singing your choice of song, particularly if you are a nonmusical bovine like yours very moo-ly, it may serve you and your nerves to bring your own accompanist. Your accompanist knows what intro and what tempo you prefer, and you know exactly how he or she plays the song. I used to bring my own accompanist, and I always felt comfortable. I vividly remember one time when I did not bring her, and I had to start my ballad over three times because I couldn't find the first note. (Little did I know that my accompanist had been adding my first note to the intro to help me out.)

Whatever happens in the audition room, no matter how badly it goes, do not project your unhappiness onto those in the room. Even if the piano player was playing with his elbows, even if the director spent the entire time texting, even if everyone on the other side of the table seemed bored to tears, be upbeat, be gracious, be professional. Which brings us to . . .

In the Audition Room

Auditions are fearsome for many people. That's a given. What you may not understand is that the folks on the other side of the table are just as fearful as you. Maybe more so.

You are hoping to get the job or at least not embarrass yourself; but if they don't choose you, you will have other job opportunities, maybe even the same week or the same day. Authors and directors work on projects sometimes for months, frequently for years. When the project finally gets off the ground and the day comes on which they have to find the right people (Four? Ten? Twenty?) to say those words and tell that story, their anxiety is through the roof.

So, your job is to convey the message, "Relax. Worry about the other roles if you want, but this part is handled." You want to present yourself as the reassuring answer to that particular casting question: professional, talented, inventive, responsive, and fun to be with.

Your audition starts the moment you walk through the door. You want to project self-confidence, professionalism, and a pleasant disposition. Smile. Make eye contact. Say hello. If they initiate a handshake, fine, but don't initiate handshakes yourself. Respond to any questions asked of you, succinctly—and with humor if you can. Speaking of humor, a sense of humor is a godsend in the Business. A humorous remark can go a long way toward breaking the ice, putting your auditors in a good, receptive mood, and relaxing yourself. A good joke or humorous remark will go a long way toward lifting you up above the rest of the sea of auditioning actors.

MADDIE'S POSITIVE ATTITUDE IS SO INTENSE IT OFTEN MELTS READERS AT AUDITIONS.

A few words of caution: one man's meat is another man's poison. A joke that bombs will do nothing to lighten the mood, and it will increase your own tension. Speaking of bombs, as fun as it may be to tease and razz your friends, an audition is the last place to humorously refer to a director or producer's less-than-successful past effort. Also, it is nowhere so true as in an audition that brevity is the soul of wit. Even if you *know* that you have great material, that you are killing it, save the routine for your standup. Your auditors are busy people. They are there not to have a bunch of yucks but to cast a show.

If you are auditioning for a television or film role, memorize the lines you have been given. You can hold the sides in your hand if you choose, but memorize your lines. If you are being put on tape, the casting director will indicate where to sit or stand. Play your lines to the casting director or whoever is reading the lines with you, not to the camera. You will be asked to slate (state your name) and then go into the scene. On camera, less is more: frenetic movement and stentorian voices are out of place. Let the camera do some of the work; simply thinking the intention is sometimes all that's needed.

If you are auditioning for a stage project, by all means hold the script. Even if you know your lines cold, hold the script so that your work is judged as an audition, not a performance. Wait until you have your auditors' attention and they have given you the go-ahead, then take your preparation and do your piece. By "take your preparation," I mean take the briefest of moments to remind yourself of the given circumstances, what just happened, to whom you are speaking, and what you want from them. You can do this by dropping your gaze momentarily to the floor and, when you are ready to start, bringing your eyes up to look at the person—imaginary or real—that you are addressing. (I find the choice of turning your back on the auditors then turning back to start your audition to be a little hokey, but if that is what works for you, do it.)

If you are singing a song, bring the sheet music over to the accompanist. Greet him or her with a smile (you want this person on your side). Go over the music. Specifically, point out where you want them to start and where you want them to finish. Do you want the full intro? Two bars? A bell tone? An arpeggio? Are you doing the song as written? Once through? Repeating the last eight measures? Are there any fermatas or "railroad tracks" you have added for your interpretation? Have you altered the lyrics? Most importantly, what tempo do you want? Hum or sing a few bars very softly to the accompanist at the tempo you want.

The music you give the accompanist should be what you plan to sing. That may seem obvious, but rehab facilities are full of accompanists driven to drink by singers who expect them to jump from bar 42 and then back from bar 64 to bar 17 and, God help us, take the whole piece down half a step. Accompanists are by and large extraordinary musicians. Do not impose on their musicianship by asking them to transpose a song on the fly. If you love the song, but it is a little high or a little low for you, pay to have someone create fresh sheet music with the transposition.

Sheet music—the actual physical sheet music—has two key requirements for the accompanist: it must stay on the piano and the pages must be easy to turn. Loose, standard-weight 8 1/2" x 11" pages are unacceptable. (They will inevitably end up on the audition room floor and you will be singing the climax of your song a cappella while your auditors write notes such as "Unprofessional," "No," and "WTF?!") A soft-cover bound volume of a musical's musical selections is okay. A loose-leaf notebook with the individual sheet music pages in see-through plastic sheets is fine. Some tech-savvy folks bring an iPad to display their music. (Just be sure it won't go into sleep mode during the audition.) Another method is to copy the sheet music onto oak-tag or other postcard-weight paper, then to tape these sheets together with a long vertical strip of scotch tape on both sides, leaving a slight gap between the joined sheets so that the sheets can be easily folded together or accordion-style. (Write your name on the music or the notebook: it is easy in the excitement/anxiety of the audition process to walk out of the room without your music.)

Speaking of anxiety, keep it to yourself. When you have finished your scene or song or monologue, take a breath or a moment and turn to your auditors with a calm, pleased expression. "That went well. What else can I show you?" is what you want to convey, whether your audition was totally nailed or epically failed. Even if you forgot the words, hit the wrong notes, and/or skipped a section, do not betray your disappointment or unhappiness with any sort of word or expression. Maybe they didn't notice. Maybe they liked it anyway. Do not instigate or reinforce any negative interpretations of what you just did. Never complain, never explain. The same goes for excuses before you start an audition. Do not tell your auditors about your cold, your lack of sleep, your four-hour travel time, your just having learned the piece, and so forth. You want to project, "I'm pretty damned good, huh?" rather than "I know I wasn't that good, but . . ."

So you turn to your auditors with a calm, pleased expression. They will either a) ask you a question or two about yourself, your background, your training, your experience; b) ask you to read or sing something else; or c) thank you for your audition. Once they thank you, nod and thank them, take your possessions (sheet music, handbag, coat, pet monkey) and take your leave.

Maintain your equanimity all the way to the elevator and out onto the street; do not exult (or moan) in sight of any of the casting assistants or other people auditioning. Once you are a couple blocks away, you can indulge in a scream of joy or despair, a fist pump or a sob of disappointment. (A corollary to this is criticizing a show you have just seen: the rule is "Never say anything negative about a show until you are at least two blocks away." Producers, writers, and so forth may well be loitering under the marquee; they will not take kindly to your breezy dismissal of their heart's blood, and they will remember you.)

Letting Go of Your Audition

If you are anything like me, you will barely have time to breathe before your mind is saying, "What I *should* have done is . . ." (The French call this *L'esprit d'escalier*—staircase wit: thinking of the perfect remark/reply only on your way out.) Maybe your second thought is a good idea, maybe not. If it is, maybe you'll get another shot at the material. In truth, second-guessing yourself is rarely profitable. The best thing to do is to study the material thoroughly; make strong, bold, truthful choices; go into the audition room; and play those choices. Then let it go. At that point, it is in the lap of the gods (or at least the casting director) and nothing you say or do will change things. So, move on. Next!

An excellent and useful way to approach auditions is to see them as a chance to give others the gift of your ideas and talent rather than as a supplication, an entreaty for others to give you a job. This is an approach advocated by Bryan Cranston, and it seems to have worked fairly well for him.

The truth is that every audition is a chance to act, to try your skills. It's a challenge, but it's also an opportunity—and not just an opportunity to get a job. It is an opportunity to *do* what you love to do, in front of an interested audience. See the value of the process. There is a reward in simply getting to work on the material, not just if you receive an offer to do the material for money in the future. Bring yourself, your skills, and your best ideas to the audition. Whether they like it or not is outside your control. Once you have left the audition room, your job is done.

Let the audition go. You have given them your gift. You have done your job; now it is time for your auditors to do theirs. Maybe they will love your gift, maybe not. Maybe you were fantastic, but you reminded the director of the cousin he hated growing up, so . . . no job offer. (I am convinced that many of the people for whom I have auditioned were traumatized by tall, blond men in their childhood.)

There is nothing to gain from rehashing, second-guessing, reliving, Monday-morning-quarterbacking your audition, so put it behind you and move forward. Elite athletes have the ability to fail (sometimes spectacularly) and put that failure behind them to succeed the next time. No matter how important the audition seemed, no matter how critical to your acting future this role seemed, the sun will come up tomorrow and there is another audition coming down the pike. Move forward.

I have found it amusing (and useful) to look back through my date book (all actors once kept hard-copy diaries for their appointments) at the six-months-earlier auditions that had seemed so important, so all-consuming at the time and which I now barely remembered. Don't waste time bemoaning lost chances, failed auditions, and roads not taken. None of us knows the future. What seems like a failure, a loss, a disaster may turn out to be the necessary step for some future triumph. I once turned down George in *Sunday in the Park with George* at San Francisco's ACT in order to do an off-Broadway musical which turned out to be a critically maligned flop. Clearly, when one compares the material, I had made a terrible choice. However, doing a show in town meant I was available to audition for other things, and I not only booked another off-Broadway show which transferred to Broadway, I booked my first feature film. Had I gone to San Francisco, neither of those things would have happened.

TV and Radio Commercials

Television and radio commercials, though not on the endangered list like soap operas, are a much different industry than they were when I began doing them 40 years ago. Back then, 75 percent or more of the on-camera commercials were shot in and around NYC, and voiceovers—and to a lesser extent, radio commercials—were almost exclusively done by a relative handful of a few dozen voice actors. (In this one specific instance, the Business *was* a rep company, with commercial producers and casting folk turning again and again to the same few versatile voice actors.) There was excellent money to be made, and while many of these actors did stage, film, and TV work in addition to these commercials, some focused exclusively on their commercial work.

"I get a lot of voice-over work. On-camera, not so much."

It's a different landscape today, as a result of changes in the broadcast industry, changes in technology, and two long, difficult strikes—the 1987 NABET (National Association of Broadcast Engineers and Technicians) strike and the 2000 SAG strike. Today, perhaps 25 percent of the on-camera commercials are shot in NYC; many are done outside the country, and a growing number of both on-camera and voice work is being done non-union. There is still excellent money to be made—occasionally—and far, far fewer actors are making an upper-middle-class livelihood from commercials.

But there is still commercial work to be had. Almost all commercial work is cast through commercial agents. There are a handful of big agencies in NY—Paradigm, CESD, Don Buchwald, Innovative, and so forth—and a similar number in LA, as well as dozens of smaller agencies in both cities. Agencies work primarily (and some work exclusively) with signed clients, but some agencies work with unsigned/freelance clients and most will send actors in whom they are interested out on a few calls to get some feedback from casting directors before signing them.

Commercial auditions are lower key than legit auditions; although the money to be made may be significant, getting the job or not will have little impact on your career and is generally no particular reflection on your abilities as an actor. Where once most advertising agencies had in-house casting directors, now the work is almost exclusively farmed out to independent casting people or casting houses.

If it is an on-camera commercial, you dress appropriately (remember: don't challenge the client's imagination unnecessarily) and show up at your call time. You fill out a line on the SAG sign-in sheet: name, agency, SAG # or Social Security # (most security-conscious actors just put "available"), call time, time in, time out, initials and then a series of check-offs: over 40/ under 40, male/female, Asian/Black/Caucasian. You pick up "the copy"—a sheet of paper detailing what happens and what (if anything) is said in the commercial. There may also be a "storyboard"—the shot-by-shot depiction comic-book style of what will be seen in the spot—either attached to the copy or (more likely) taped to the wall above the sign-in sheet. Read the copy assiduously, picking up any clues you can for your audition. Memorize (if you can) your lines. There will probably be a cue card, a large sheet of oaktag with the dialogue printed on it, on a stand next to the camera in the audition room—but it's always best not to have to be reading your lines.

When you are called into the room, stand at the opposite side of the room from the camera, a couple feet from the wall. (There will probably be some tape on the floor—this is your "mark.") The casting person will ask you to "slate:" you look in the camera, smile, and state your name. You will do the little scene. The casting person may give you some feedback/direction and ask you to do the scene again. (Listen very carefully to that direction, and even if you disagree with it, do your damnedest to give them what they asked for.) Fill in your "time out" on the sign-in sheet and the initials box (if you haven't already initialed it), and you're done.

Voiceover (VO) and radio auditions have similarities with one gratifying exception: you can look like anything you want (no need to dress up, put on makeup, or shave.) You sign in, pick up your copy, and wait to be called in. You will audition in a recording booth, which may be an actual soundproof little room separate from the room where the casting person is, or a makeshift lean-to in the corner of the same room. Adjust the mike so that it is pointing at your nose and about three inches from your mouth. Hold your copy up at eye level, or if they have a music stand, raise the stand and fold the top of the copy over the top of the music stand so that your first line is the first thing visible.

Some radio spots are an interaction between you and another person. Simple enough: just do the scene, playing off the other person and speaking into the microphone. Voiceovers and spokesperson or solo radio spots are slightly different.

You will slate at the casting director's hand gesture and then "read" the copy. I put *read* in quotes because the voiceover client doesn't want a herald reading some pronouncement. You are speaking to one person. Figure out who that specific person is for you and why you are saying these particular words to him or her. (Sound familiar? The same questions you ask yourself in a legit audition, except you can personalize them—not Antigone speaking to Creon, but a woman talking to her dad.)

There are various tricks and gimmicks of the craft. Literally smile when you say the name of the product or the client. "Billboard" the last line—that is, lay out the words with particular distinction and emphasis: this is what you want your listener to remember. Actively listen to the voiceovers you hear on TV, and you will rapidly begin to get a grasp of the standard rhythms and approaches to voiceovers. If you think this is a good field for you, there are a number of coaches/teachers who will give you the basic pointers and even assist you in creating a voiceover reel. (This reel will feature you doing snippets of various spots that your VO teacher will have recorded on a couple of different microphones in a couple of different recording booths so as to give the impression that you were actually hired to do these commercials.)

7

Sherpas, Guides, and Trail Masters

Representation and Representing

Finding an Agent

If there is one question that I get all the time, it is "How can I get an agent?" It is an understandable query. Agents seem to hold the magic key to career opportunities. And there is some undeniable truth to that perception. An agent receives a "breakdown"—a description of the roles a production is looking to fill—and from their roster of represented clients, the agent sends the casting person their suggestions for each role. The casting person then says yes or no to the various suggestions, setting up audition appointments for the yesses.

For stage work, while Actors' Equity mandates auditions for Broadway shows and some other contracts through their Equity Principal Auditions and Equity Chorus Calls, not all contracts have these required calls. And some, if not many, of the roles may already be cast through readings, prior productions, or a director's personal connections. And if you are not yet a member of Equity, your chance of being seen at these auditions is slim indeed. And then there is the world of SAG-AFTRA work—film, episodic TV, commercials, voiceovers, and so forth—which is almost exclusively cast through agent submissions.

If you examine the description of breakdowns, you may notice at least two cracks through which your potential audition opportunity may slip even if you have an agent. Your agents may not feel that you are right for a role (remember my not getting submitted for Miles Gloriosus?) or may feel that they have someone else or a couple of someone elses who are "more right" for the role. So you may have representation, but you may not be submitted.

And—second crack—even if you are submitted, the casting representative may not agree to see you. (This is where you want an agent who believes passionately in you, because most agents, if they submit three actors for a role and get two appointments, will declare victory and not push for the third actor.)

All this, of course, reflects the difference between one's own assessment of one's skills and abilities and the Business's point of view. Remember how I said the Business was not a rep company, that they didn't need astonishing chameleon-like jacks of all trades? In order to make sense of the tens and tens of thousands of professional actors, the Business necessarily pigeonholes actors according to their type, their strong suit, their most salient feature. Casting folks do this, and even your agents do this. So although you may look at many different character descriptions that aren't quite you and say, "Hey, I could do that!" (because hey, you *could*), your agent and certainly the casting director are likely to be less offbeat/inventive/off-center in their choice of those auditioning.

So here is where perseverance, tenacity, and assertiveness come into play. If you think this is your role—even if the description misses you by five years or four inches or twenty pounds—do whatever you can to get yourself in that room. Bug your agent. Bug the casting director. Camp outside the audition room. A word of caution: don't make a pest of yourself unless it's the right role and you have the goods; otherwise you will merely have created a strong impression as a pain in the butt who wastes people's time. But certainly don't be shy, standoffish, and overly polite. As a former Freddy Eynsford-Hill, I can tell you, faint heart never won my fair lady. And frequently the director himself doesn't know exactly what he wants until he sees it, which is why casting directors sometimes "cast" a wide net.

In the mid-'90s, I was doing a new musical up at the Berkshire Theatre Festival. Pat McCorkle, who had cast me in the musical, got the job to cast the latest *Die Hard* movie, then known as *Die Hard New York* or simply *Die Hard 3*, but eventually called *Die Hard with a Vengeance*. (I still remember the giddy enthusiasm with which director John McTiernan shared this new title with me. It left me cold then and now.) Pat asked me to audition for one of the gang of bad guys. She put all the potential bad guys on tape reading the same few lines belonging to the No. 2 bad guy, one Matthias Targo. Targo was described in the script as "mid 30s, small, dark; he never smiles." A week or so later, I was thrilled when my agent called to tell me I had been cast in the movie. "Great! What role am I playing?"

"The one you auditioned for."

"Yeah, but which one of the bad guys am I playing?"

"The one you auditioned for."

It took several of these "Who's on first?" exchanges before this 6'5" blond who was 45 years old and smiled a lot understood that the director's vision of Targo had trumped the screenwriter's vision of Targo.

Of course, I might have been the absolute embodiment of Targo, but if I didn't have an agent, I almost certainly would never have been seen for the role. So agents are important—particularly for film and TV—and if you don't have one, how do you get one?

In the frustratingly difficult world of Show Business, acquiring an agent is its own special little nexus of frustration. It is akin to the search for the One, the guy or gal with whom you wish to spend the rest of your life. It may seem like a hopeless bramble of false starts and dead ends, but most people end up with a spouse, and many actors end up with an agent. If you don't have representation, keep looking for one and keep creating opportunities for an agent to see you and your work. Even if you have representation, keep creating opportunities for you and your work to be seen.

It sometimes seems like a Catch 22: the best way to get good work is with an agent, and the best way to get an agent is with good work. I strongly advocate that, rather than throwing up your hands at this paradox, you use it to inspire your simultaneous efforts on a two-fold path: finding good work and finding an agent. Network, schmooze, and investigate in your efforts to find work opportunities. Network, schmooze, and investigate in your efforts to find an agent.

Taking a page from our acting handbook on understanding and creating a character, let's look at this from the agent's point of view. Like actors, agents have varying levels of success. There are powerhouse agencies (William Morris, Endeavor, CAA, UTA). There are mid-level agencies; there are boutique agencies; there are startup agencies. There are superstar agents, and there are mid-level agents and beginning agents and junior agents and wannabe-agent mail clerks.

As an agent, you get 10 percent of what your client makes, but since unlike some of your clients, you're not going to be tending bar (we hope) to make ends meet, and you have rent and other expenses, you need more than ten clients to make a living. Let's say your agency has three agents and a receptionist: you'll need 100 to 120 clients or about two for every age between 18 and 68. You might have more clients in their late 20s to early 40s, because that is probably the sweet spot of employment.

When it comes to picking or adding clients, you as the agent ask yourself two questions: 1) what is the likely payoff in increased income for me versus the increased expense of my bandwidth, the time I have to spend on promoting and caring for this client? and 2) does this person fill a gap in my client roster or does he or she basically duplicate someone I already have? It is like building an investment portfolio: you want return on investment and a diversification of holdings.

For actors over 50, the answers are rarely promising: the actor is not a candidate for breakout status and has reached an age of fewer opportunities. Also, the agent likely already has similar actors in this category, actors for whom the agent may already be hard-pressed to find work. (At some point in my mid- to late-50s, feeling under-appreciated by my representation, I investigated the possibility of new agents. Nobody was very keen to take me on—and I'm an actor who works a lot and makes money!)

Actors in their mid-career (30s and 40s) are more easily employable, but an agent may well have that category filled. What causes gaps in an agent's roster is the churning of clients as actors jump from one agent to another. You may say to yourself, "My career is going nowhere—I need a new agent." Perhaps you then sign with Agent X, who has an opening because they just lost your competition (Actor A) to Agency Y because Y lost Actor B who signed with your old agency. And so it goes.

Hypothetically, an actor—let's call him Wick Nyman—may feel that there is this other actor—let's call him Gictor Varber—who gets all Wick's roles. Boy, Wick says, if I had *his* agent, I'd be working all the time. So Wick signs with Gictor's agent. Gictor still gets the auditions for Wick's roles and the roles themselves, and Wick doesn't. The roles Gictor doesn't want? Wick doesn't want them either. This hypothetical situation is, of course, a complete fabrication and bears no resemblance to the events of the late '70s and early '80s surrounding the Agency for the Performing Arts.

All this is to say that switching agents is not necessarily the solution to your problems. Part of the mission of this book is to get you to take responsibility for your career and your life in the Business and give you some tools and guidance to help you do so.

If you are at the beginning of that career, there is some good news: people keep getting older. Meryl Streep is not going to play Juliet. The Business always needs new young actors. Agents always need new young actors. If you are a new young actor, congratulations! You are in the sweet spot. The third category of agent clients—18- to 28-year-old actors—always needs to be restocked.

So, if you are an agent, where do you get those new young actors? You can browse the young actors in TV shows, feature films, and Broadway productions, but those actors will probably already have an agent, and if not, you will lose them to a behemoth such as William Morris.

You can browse the actors in showcase productions or Off-Off-Broadway or 99-seat-theatre productions. This is unbelievably time consuming (you could go the theatre every night of the year in NY or LA and still not see all the shows), and the quality of the work is wildly uneven. Most agents try to catch a few of these shows (especially, of course, the ones their current clients are doing) and also ask their assistants and subagents to catch others.

A better use of an agent's time is to scout potential clients at a "senior showcase." No, this is not a festival for geriatric thespians. Theatre programs showcase their graduating actors in an afternoon or evening of scenes and songs for an audience of agents and casting directors. Where once there were less than a dozen elite programs and all their final-year students performed in one marathon session known as "the Leagues," now there are dozens and dozens of reputable programs, and their senior showcases can cause a scheduling headache each spring.

Lastly, there are the more anomalous situations. A family friend asks you to meet their nephew. A client recommends someone they did a reading with. An acting teacher friend has a pupil they think highly of. You attend a "pay to play" showcase evening where a dozen actors have ponied up money to some institute for the chance to show you what they can do.

"The good news is you got the part. The bad news is I have no idea who I'm talking to."

So this is what it looks like from the agent's POV: these are the possible ways for you, the agent, to get new clients. The best way is those senior show-cases because the age of the actors fills your greatest need and they have all had extensive training. The downside is that there is a lot of competition for the most employable actors. And that is the key metric: employability—not necessarily, and certainly not *just*, talent, but employability. Just as there are certain types of actors you the agent really need and other types you can pass over, there are certain types of actors that the Business always wants and needs (and others who have to do a little more clawing on their way up the ladder of success). And remember, that is what an agent wants from a new client:

someone who makes them money, gives them a good return in time and energy invested, and/or fills a gap in their roster.

Now that you have looked at this situation from the agent's POV, we can better craft your approach to getting an agent. Remember what I said about big agencies, boutique agencies, and startup agencies? You need to decide whether you want a big, powerful agency where you might get lost or a smaller office that might not have as much clout to get you seen. And you need to be right-sized about your choice. If you are just starting out, CAA is not going to want to have anything to do with you. You want an agency that represents people at your level of the Business. If you are a SAG or Equity member, you can go to the union's office and look at a printout of various agencies' clients to see who represents folks like you. If you are not yet a union member, you can browse through *Players Directory* to see who is representing your peers. (*Players Directory*, published by Now Casting, is a thick book of actors' headshots and their contact/representation information, arranged by type—Leading Man, Character Man, Juvenile, and so forth. You must be a union actor to be listed in the *Directory*; when you get your card, you will want to be in *Players Directory*.)

When you approach an agent, you don't want to be an arrogant jerk (that's my job), but you do want to be the Answer, not the Question. You want to be the person who says to an agent, "I am who you are missing, and I will make you money." To that end, you will need to take a look at your attributes. Remember when we discussed what you are selling? (Your long suit? Your type? Your roles?) Now we're going to market you.

Are you gorgeous? If so, great—you have just lapped the rest of the field. Are you brilliant at comedy? If so, great—you have just sprinted to the head of the field. If you are gorgeous and brilliant at comedy, give this book to a friend: you will not need to hunt for an agent, you will need to hunt for a financial advisor.

Gorgeousness opens a lot of doors, particularly for women. Simply sending a headshot and accompanying note will get you an interview with most agents. Young women in television, film, and plays are almost invariably described as knockouts. If you are a very attractive young woman, an agent is going to see dollar signs. The agent's only question is "Can she act?" That is where your résumé serves as reassurance, either because of the roles you have done and the places you have done them, or because of the school or training program you graduated from, or because of the freelance acting teachers you have studied with.

If you are not gorgeous, join the club. And weep no tears. Most of us can pass for sufficient gorgeousness from the back of a 1,000-seat theatre or with the help of the magicians in the makeup department. Do what you can to let your particular beauty flourish: eat right, drink plenty of water, exercise. Clear eyes, full hearts, can't lose—as *Friday Night Lights* has it. So make sure you're not undermining your own gorgeousness, and then let it go.

The other big question an agent will have is "Can this person act? If I get them in the door, will they deliver?" To answer this question, an agent relies on firsthand and secondhand information. Firsthand is where the agent sees you perform—and we'll get back to that. Secondhand is where the agent relies on what he or she reads or hears about you.

Your headshot and résumé are the major sources of secondhand information about you. Your photo should say professional: well lit, in focus, the correct size, and attached firmly to your résumé. Your photo should be flattering, but above all should look like you and project who you are. Your résumé should include every potentially positive scrap of relevant, truthful info. That is why you want to include credits that reflect well upon the extent of your experience, the breadth of your experience, the quality of the places you have worked, and the notable and reputable people you have worked with. Impressive is what you want, but intriguing and interesting and amusing are all good as well. You want to use this second-hand info to get yourself through the door, in the room, in front of this person, so that you can personally dazzle him or her firsthand with your skills and charm. So yes, if Steven Spielberg came and talked to your class, definitely shoehorn him into your training credits somehow. But also include the wacky, the weird, and/or the giggle inducing. Christopher Durang grew up in the next town over from me, and we did summer theatre together. While playing Mr. Sowerberry to my Fagin in 1969, he filmed a zany adaptation of *The Brothers Karamazov* in which I as Fyodor was attacked with an eggbeater by one of my sons and, sadly, eggbeaten to death. My first film credit and a golden conversation piece.

The best way for your headshot and résumé to land on an agent's desk—Plan A—is for Joe Mantello or Jack O'Brien to burst through the agent's door and say, slamming your headshot on the desk, "You have *got* to see this person!"

Plan B, which is more likely, is to have someone the agent knows recommend you to the agent. Unless the person knows you well, this can also be problematic, as people are generally unwilling to stake their artistic reputation and/or their relationship with the agent on a single performance or brief encounter. Most people, however, are amenable to being referenced in a more noncommittal fashion, as in "So-and-so saw me in a showcase/did a play reading with me/had lunch together recently, and he suggested I get in touch with you." A perfectly valid form of this is the laying out of a personal connection, however tenuous: "My Uncle Morty was your camp counselor." "My mother went to high school with you." Once again, you want some point of reference that will lift your headshot and résumé a few inches above the flood tide of unsolicited headshots that arrive at an agent's office daily.

When you send your headshot and résumé in—ideally, preceded by someone's recommendation—you will also send a little cover letter or note, preferably referencing that known third party who suggested your get in touch with the agent. That cover letter is a further chance to lift yourself above the crowd.

Remember the two advantageous attributes I singled out? Looking good and being funny. If you are good at being funny, here is your chance to shine. Just like a cat video or some other internet meme, a humorous note is more likely to be forwarded on by an agent's first line of defense, the assistant who opens the mail. Funny is money.

If you can't be funny, be charming. (If you can be both funny and charming, that's golden.) Whatever level of humor or charm the note contains, it needs to make a couple of key points: you are looking for representation and you will call the agent in a week or so to set up a face-to-face visit. (Don't suggest he call you; tell him you will call.) These are the essentials. Mention the reference or the recommendation if you have one. If there is an upcoming opportunity to see your work—showcase, fringe festival, TV show, 99-seat theatre, short film festival, whatever—by all means let the agent know about it. If you have good, clear handwriting, a hand-written note (on stationery, not on a ripped-out sheet of notebook paper) is fine, otherwise type it.

Having sent the headshot, résumé and cover letter, and having told the agent that you would call in a week, what should you do? Call in a week! When the receptionist answers, say "This is [Your Name Here], calling for [Important Agent]." The receptionist will probably put you through to the agent's assistant. If the receptionist asks what this is in reference to, tell him or her that you and the agent are trying to firm up an appointment.

When you reach the agent's assistant, make sure you get the agent's assistant's name. Let's say his name is Cody. Addressing him or her by name, you state your connection: "Hey, Cody, I just did a reading with [Signed Client]/my dad and [Important Agent] were fraternity brothers/my aunt was [Important Agent]'s dance teacher, and [he/she] suggested I get in touch with [Important Agent]." Tell Cody that you sent a photo and résumé last week with a cover letter and you are calling to find out when might be a good time for a meeting with the important agent.

Now here's the thing about Cody. He is probably grossly underpaid (because there are far more people who want to be in Show Business than there are jobs in Show Business), but what salary he does receive is paid for exactly two reasons: getting a hold of the important people the agent wants to talk to and keeping at bay the less important people who want to talk to the agent. So Cody's job is not to connect you with the important agent; in fact, his job is to not connect you to the important agent.

If Cody is good at his job, he will say "[Important Agent] is with a client/ on a call/in a meeting right now, but I will let him know you called. What's the best number to reach you at?" This is, to paraphrase Touchstone, the Reproof Valiant. Thank Cody, give him your number, and ask him to tell [Important Agent] that [Personal Connection] says hi. Take out your contacts notebook and write on the page of the important agent the date you mailed the headshot, the date of the phone call, what transpired on the call, and how it was left.

Call the agency in three to five days and say to the receptionist, "This is [Your Name Here]. [Important Agent]'s assistant Cody—what's his last name again?" (Write down his full name on IA's page in your contacts notebook.) "Oh right. Would you please put me through to him?" When you reach Cody, tell him you spoke the previous week, remind him of the personal connection and ask if you might talk to the important agent about setting up a meeting. Cody will probably come up with another creative brushoff. Thank him and leave your number. Pick up a sheet of stationery and write a note to Cody c/o the talent agency acknowledging him for what a good job he is doing protecting the important agent. Tell him he will be doing IA an even bigger favor by allowing you to meeting IA because you plan to make IA some serious coin.

In the Room with the Agent

Let us say you have successfully begged, bribed, cajoled, charmed, or some-thing-elsed your way into a meeting. Let's make it a successful one. Dress tastefully in (probably) business casual. If your type is a dese/dem/dose blue collar guy who wouldn't be caught dead in a tie, you can put on a blue chambray shirt and a clean pair of chinos. You can shade the business casual toward an outfit more suitable to your long suit, but most of the time, you can't go wrong in business casual.

Give yourself sufficient time to get to the appointment so that bad traffic or transit snafus won't throw you, even if it means you have to kill a little time outside the building/office. Arrive at the office a little early (5–10 minutes), and tell the receptionist that you have a 4:30 (or whatever) appointment with the important agent. Get the receptionist's name and be friendly and charming (because the receptionist may be running a studio in 10 years.) If an assistant comes out to get you, ask their name, and thank them if you had any telephone or email colloquy with them.

Once in the room, thank the agent, and settle in for a bravura performance of "The Interview." Interviewing is nearly as important a skill as auditioning—the trail to many jobs/opportunities in the Business either begins or ends with an interview—and you will want to be as well prepared for an interview as you are for an audition. "But," you may say, "how can I prepare for an interview?" Stop whimpering and I'll tell you.

The agent will want to know about your background, training, and experience. He or she might pick up much of this from your résumé, but the agent wants more than the cut-and-dried, black-and-white bare bones of the tale your résumé tells—he or she wants to get to know you: what you're like as a person, what your personality is like, what you are like to be with. So your job is to be a delightful person with a charming personality who is fun to be with.

How to be charming and delightful? The saying is, "if you want to be interesting, be interested." If there is something unusual in the agent's office, ask about it. If the office or the decor or the location is really cool, comment favorably on it. If the agent is wearing some article of clothing you admire, say so. Don't be a transparently toadying, sycophantic suck-up, but remember that a little flattery never hurts.

Many of the agent's questions will be predictable: Where did you go to school? Where did you grow up? Other possible questions are less predictable: What casting agents do you know? How do you see yourself? Where do you see yourself in five years? Prepare these answers so as to be both informative and engaging/entertaining. Your job is not just to satisfy the agent's request for knowledge; it is also to leave a positive impression in the agent's mind. You want to be remembered, to raise your profile above the sea of other actors.

You may dream of going on a late-night talk show to promote your latest blockbuster movie. In the Johnny Carson era (before talk show appearances became so blatantly tied to plugging movies or TV shows), actors would have their Johnny Carson Story—the anecdote they would tell if they ever got on Johnny's show. Polish up your own Johnny Carson Story: it is now your Agent Story. You want something interesting that leaves a good impression; it could be hilarious or touching or self-deprecating or heroic or any number of things. It should be brief. (Tales of hilarity and heroism wear thin after a minute.). Figure out a few different segues into the story so that you can interpolate this tale into your Agent conversation without some lame "Hey, let me tell you about the time . . ." intro.

Johnny' s people never called my people, so I never got to tell my JCS. You will hear it here first:

My first year in New York, I was cast out of an open call in a workshop of a new musical called *Philemon* by Tom Jones and Harvey Schmidt. I was out-of-my-mind excited to be working with Broadway actors such as Susan Watson, Keith Charles, and Leila Martin. The first day of rehearsal, Tom Jones explained to us that the royalties for *The Fantasticks* were no longer what they once were, and as much as he would like to pay us all handsome salaries, there would instead be an honorarium of $250. My brain and self-esteem were so addled that I spent the next several minutes casting about mentally for people from whom I could borrow $250 to pay Tom and Harvey for the privilege of being in their show.

Prepare your JCS. Prepare your answers to the obvious questions and my suggested less-obvious ones. Then pause to consider the other side of the equation. It is not just about what the agent wants to know about you; it is also what you want this agent to know about you.

Take a cue from the political candidates you see during a debate. When asked a question, they frequently answer not the question asked but rather the question they wish had been asked; they produce their preferred sound bite, they stay "on message." I am not suggesting that you be nonresponsive or evasive in answering an agent's inquiries. I am suggesting that you figure out what you want the agent to know about you and then, once you are in the room, figure out a way to introduce that info into the conversation. What things about you would be useful things to share? What might you tell this person that will differentiate you from the dozens of other actors they will interview and make them remember you?

And after the interview, however it went, thank the agent for seeing you. Go home and write them a charming thank-you note. If the agent's agency is interested in you, you will hear from them. If you don't hear from them . . . well, in the world of Show Business, no news is not good news. It is possible that the agent actually liked you, but their agency felt they already had enough of your type, so while you continue to search for representation, you might drop the agent a line when some good news happens for you. But remember, no news is not good news—so don't send the agent a postcard saying, "Hey, how are you doing? Nothing's happening. Just wanted to keep in touch." Good news is a job, a class, or an opportunity to be seen.

Marketing Yourself/Self-Promotion

As you can tell from the foregoing, getting an agent to meet with you—let alone represent you—on the basis of secondhand information is an uphill battle. Seeing is believing, they say, and since you want an agent who believes in you, it will behoove you to be seen by your prospective agent. There is a school of thought that says you should grab every opportunity, that you should work whenever you can just to put yourself out there. Undeniably, not being seen is less effective than being seen. And seen. And scene.

The best way to be seen is in a great role in a wonderful high-profile production. E. Katherine Kerr (who was simply Elaine Kerr when I played her jockey-brief-clad inamorata in her own play *Juno's Swans* at Ensemble Studio Theatre in the '70s) used to say that, in order to break through, you had to be good in a good role in a good production. This was after Katherine's breakthrough role as the mother in Tommy Tune's wonderful Off-Broadway production of *Cloud Nine*. The corollary rule is that it's not good enough to do a great role in a mediocre production or a forgettable role in a great production (or to play opposite a tall blond guy dressed in a pair of tighty whities.)

But this rule of thumb is for breaking through, not breaking in. If you are good in *either* a good role or a good production, you have something that is worth seeing. (If you are *not* good in the show and/or the show is truly terrible, this performance should definitely not be an agent or a casting person's first impression of you. You're only new once.) The trick is getting an agent to come. The most likely avenue of success is piggybacking on someone else's representation. If someone in your show already has an agent, ask them to encourage their agent to come. Find out when the agent is coming and send the agent a note afterwards—or even before.

Even if no one has an agent, put it out there to prospective agents and casting people. Write them a charming funny note or email letting them know when the show is, why they should come see it and offering to arrange tickets for them. (Most showcases/fringe shows/99-seat theatres offer complimentary tickets for agents and casting people as a professional courtesy.) Start early. Follow up. Send a second and third letter/email. People forget. They get busy. Other plans fall through. Plans change. Put yourself and your production in the forefront of their mind. Even if they don't come (and—spoiler alert— most agents and casting folks will ignore your pleas), you will have raised your profile and put yourself in their consciousness. You will be one step higher than the rest of the flood of thespian humanity that is your competition.

Here, as examples of a self-promotion campaign, are my efforts to get NYC casting folks to come see me suffer in 1996 with Byron Jennings, Ben Shenkman, and Alma Cuervo and cavort in 1999 with Roger Rees, Uma Thurman, and Michael Emerson:

MCC Theater

Robert LuPone & Bernard Telsey, Executive Directors
W.D. Cantler, Associate Director

presents

"[An] intriguing and unconventional thriller (Thomson News).

"... A cunningly told, compelling spy story." (Thomson News).

"... A beguiling debate on state morality versus personal morality ...." (Toronto Star)

"A fascinating kaleidoscope of conversations ... Crackling with ideas and moral conundrums." (Now)

by **Jason Sherman**
directed by **Pamela Berlin**

with
**Fred Burrell, Alma Cuervo, Byron Jennings
Ben Shenkman, Nick Wyman**

Sets: Neil Patel
Costumes: Michael Krass
Lights: Howard Werner
Music and Sound: David Van Tieghem
Production Supervisors: Ira Mont, Bernadette McGay
Production Stage Manager: Elaine Bayless

MCC Theater is pleased to present the American premiere of THREE IN THE BACK, TWO IN THE HEAD, by Jason Sherman. This sophisticated and fast paced thriller, winner of Canada's 1995 Governor-General's Award for Drama, is the story of a son who searches the CIA for his father's murderer and is pulled deeper and deeper into a political house of mirrors that eventually shatters everything in which he once believed.

**Reservations: (212) 727-7765
Tickets $25**
Visa/MC/DC/CB

May 13 - June 8
Mondays through Saturdays at 8PM, Saturdays at 3PM
Special Opening Night Benefit: Saturday, May 18, 8PM ($50)

MCC Theater · 120 West 28th Street NYC 10001 (212)727-7765

100 Madison Avenue
Larchmont, N.Y. 10538
May 14, 1996

Dear Harve and Barry.

With the Kentucky Derby and Cinco de Mayo safely behind us, it's time to put down your juleps and Coronas and turn your attention to the next great event of the spring: the American premiere of Three in the Back, Two in the Head, winner of Canada's 1995 Governor-General's Award for Drama. (Quick--name the 1994 Governor-General's Award winner. Name any previous Governor-General's Award winner. Name the Governor-General. And you call yourself a North American.) Yes, thanks to NAFTA, the theatres of New York will soon be overrun with cheap Canadian drama while Edward Albee is forced to squeegee windshields on Twelfth Avenue. The point piece in this invasion is a nifty little (an intermissionless 90 minutes) thriller about a murdered rocket scientist who may have been working for the CIA and his son's efforts to find out the truth about his life and death. The Manitoba (formerly Manhattan) Class Company is offering you 28 chances to see this treasure over the next four weeks -- Monday through Saturday at 8:00, and Saturday afternoon at 3:00. Call for reservations at 727-7765. Come soon: Nixon's Nixon and The Grey Zone sold out fast. Hope to see you on 28th Street.

Respectfully yours,

Nick Wyman

100 Madison Avenue

Larchmont, N.Y. 10538

May 21, 1996

Dear Pat,

On this part of the CDATs (Casting Director Achievement Tests), you are asked to fill in the next item in a sequence, e.g., Pudgy, Plump, _____; Tinkers, Evers, _____. Did you get those right? Fat Chance. Now for the tough ones:

1) <u>Seven Guitars</u>, <u>Rent</u>, _____.

2) <u>Nixon's Nixon</u>, <u>The Grey Zone</u>, _____.

3) <u>Loot</u> at Hartford Stage, <u>Howard Stern's Private Parts</u>, _____.

[Hint: the categories are 1) prize-winning plays you have seen or are about to see, 2) Manhattan Class Company productions this season, and 3) Nick Wyman's latest jobs.]

The answer in all three categories is <u>Three in the Back, Two in the Head</u>, now through June 8th at MCC, 120 West 28th Street. Call 727-7765 for reservations and tell them you got a perfect 1600 on theCDATs.

Yours in perfect casting,

Nick Wyman

FINAL NOTICE

100 Madison Avenue

Larchmont, N.Y. 10538

May 29, 1996

Dear Sir:

We have sent you numerous requests to come see <u>Three in the Back, Two in the Head</u> at the Manhattan Class Company, and so far we have not received word of your attendance. No doubt it has slipped your mind. Please submit your eyes and ears to the invigorating 80-minute stimulation of this prize-winning Canadian play some Monday through Saturday night at 8:00 (or Saturday afternoon at 3:00) before the show closes on June 8th, or we will be forced to turn your account over to our audience collection agency: Bruno the Enforcer. If your presence and this missive have crossed in the mail, please accept our apologies and thank you for your patronage.

With concern,

Nick

Nick Wyman, Pres.

A.C.T.O.R.*

*(Annoying Casters Through Obnoxious Requests)

100 Madison Avenue

Larchmont, NY 10538

January 5, 1999

Dear Alexa,

1999 resolutions:

    1. Lose ten pounds.

    2. Finish screenplay.

    3. Go see Uma Thurman, Roger Rees and Nick Wyman in the hip, new translation of Moliere's <u>The Misanthrope</u> at the Classic Stage Company.

Look -- you don't really need to lose ten pounds and Harvey & Bob have all the screenplays they can use about lovable NYC casting directors. Just wear black, bag the screenplay, and call Jennifer at HWA (889-0800) to get house seats for the CSC's <u>Misanthrope</u> January 28th through February 28th.

Act fast or live in regret.

Still available for the next millenium,

Nick Wyman

100 Madison Avenue

Larchmont, NY 10538

February 2, 1999

Bernie Telsey

Bernard Telsey Casting

120 West 28th Street

New York, NY 10001

Dear Bernie,

February 2nd, 1999 – what does that day bring up for you? Perhaps Groundhog Day – and you wonder whether Punxsutawney Phil will see his shadow and whether <u>Company Man</u> will perk up Bill Murray's career. Perhaps James Joyce's birthday – and you wonder what sort of impenetrably arcane prose a half-blind, 117-year-old Irish drunk would produce.

Or perhaps all those folks who were dishing you at the last CSA convention are wrong, and February 2nd makes you say "Oh my God! Only four more weeks to see Uma Thurman, Roger Rees and Nick Wyman in Off-Broadway's hottest, hippest, cleverest comedy; and only *two* more weeks to allow me to say 'CSC's <u>The Misanthrope</u>? It's fabulous – I saw it in previews.'"

So practice that jaded, been-there-done-that insouciance, and call Jennifer at HWA (889-0800) for house seats because hey – if you miss Uma, Roger and me on stage, you might as well be in Punxsutawney.

Yours at Off-Broadway prices,

Bernie

Nick Wyman   .

Dear ,

Now that the hubbub of Shrove Tuesday is past, and you've digested all those pancakes and broken all those Lenten promises, it's time to turn your attention to your theatre-going. Specifically, when in the next ten days are you going to see Uma Thurman, Roger Rees, Michael Emerson, Mary Lou Rosato, and yours very truly in The Misanthrope at the Classic Stage Company? You only have until March 7th; and while the show is sold out, house seats are still available through Jennifer at HWA (889-0800.) Come and laugh – you won't regret it.

Yours on 13th Street,

Nick Wyman

All this assumes you are trying to get an agent to come to see a limited-run, noncommercial stage production. There are other possibilities of showcasing oneself. If you are graduating from a reputable theatre program, they may well have a senior showcase to which agents and casting folks are invited. This is a golden opportunity for two reasons: 1) whatever you are doing will be tailor made to show off your skills and (one hopes) your long suit, and 2) the whole evening is aimed toward the sweet spot of every agent's needs: talented, trained young performers.

Your school or theatre department will take care of invitations. Don't shy away from the opportunity to double down on their efforts. Send your own notes with accompanying headshot and résumé to several agents. You want to get them interested/invested in you even before the showcase.

Hang around after the showcase in the lobby/hallway with family and friends so that any interested agent or impressed casting person can speak to you. (If anyone does, get their name and memorize it.) Avoid hanging with your fellow performing seniors so that if an agent liked you but not your friend, he or she won't feel constrained about approaching you.

From your school, get the names of all the agents and casting folks who attended the showcase. Send a note (reminding them of the monologues/numbers/scenes you did in the showcase) telling them you will call to see if you can set up an interview. Allow time for the note to arrive, then call and follow the protocol I laid out earlier. As for casting folk, send them a note (once again detailing whatever it was you did in the showcase) telling them you will call to see if they would be willing to meet with you and share some advice and counsel.

If you didn't go to a school with a senior showcase and you are not appearing in a stage production anywhere, you can still give prospective agents a sample of your work by emailing them a video of yourself performing. A strong word of caution: this had better be killer. You should only send the strongest possible evidence of your abilities. A grainy, out-of-focus video taken from the balcony of your high school production of *Godspell* will do more harm than good. And video of you as a 20-year-old Abuelita in *In the Heights* or as Sir Joseph Surface in *The Rivals* will not help you. Make sure your video is of you in a contemporary piece doing a role you could do today (not in 30 years.) Make sure whatever you send represents you at your finest. Any concerns, quibbles, or second thoughts? Don't send it.

Another source of potential video on yourself are short films, particularly student films. Undergraduate and graduate film students need actors for their projects, and you can usually read about these opportunities online or on campus bulletin boards (NYU, Columbia, the New School, City College, NY Film Academy) or in the "trades." I strongly encourage you to do this work, as it will at least give you experience in front of a camera and may give you some usable film on yourself. *May* give you some usable film. Once again, think long and hard before sending a video of you as Pitti-Sing in a zombie version of *The Mikado* to an agent.

Your Web Presence/Your Brand

In this day and age of everything seeming to be discoverable and knowable on the Internet, people have changed their research and shopping habits. When was the last time you wandered down to your local library to get information about something? Probably never: it is much easier to do a web search or check out Wikipedia. How much of your Christmas shopping did you do in brick-and-mortar stores last year? Maybe less than half—and maybe much of that was after checking things out and comparing prices and models online. We get so, so much of our information online these days. So, if you want folks—including agents and directors—to find out about you, you need to be a presence on the web.

Probably you already are a presence: you probably have a Facebook account and a Twitter account and an Instagram account. You may have a Tumblr account or some other blog or a Snapchat account or a fill-in-the-blank-with-the-latest-flavor-of-social-media account. You may even have a website and/or a YouTube channel. These are your public face, and if you are going to scale the mountain of Show Business, you need to give some thought to them.

You want your public face to be wildly popular. One of the considerations that casting occasionally takes into account is your number of followers. Although there are anecdotes of people losing roles to someone else with more followers, this is usually a rather high-end issue—as in choosing which actor will best open a movie or popularize a TV show or revive a Broadway production. This is a Twitter and Instagram issue (since Facebook caps your allowable number of "friends"), so give some thought to how you curate your image on those outlets. Post things that are fun and appealing. Learn how to hashtag effectively so as to draw more eyeballs to your feed. You can become your own publicist—at a very pleasant price point.

You cannot sacrifice propriety for popularity. If an agent who is considering making you a client, or a director who is considering you for a role, looks at your FB page or your Twitter feed or your Instagram photos, what impression will they form? Hmmm. Those drunken selfies and those clever tweets trashing that director's last show might just be problematic. Consider doing a judicious edit of your posts and tweets and photos and consider tailoring your public persona from this moment on. You want to put your best foot forward. If you feel you have to let your freak flag fly in social media, consider either 1) changing the privacy settings on your account to eliminate the likelihood of John Q. Agent or Jennifer Q. Director spotting that offensive/immature photo/post, or 2) creating two separate accounts: one personal one that is tightly limited in its access to your pals and one public one that is the responsible, employable face you wish to present to the world. Since the first choice simply walls you off from those who might represent you or employ you, I strongly recommend the latter to those who feel they must have a fun-loving, trashy social media outlet in which to interact with their buddies.

As you look to promote yourself, you have two huge advantages over the actors of the last century: you have a near state-of-the-art video camera in your pocket or purse and you have a worldwide distribution network instantly available to you. If you have some cleverness, some charm, and some energy, Instagram is your best buddy. In our current age of short attention spans and preferring images to text, a steady stream of clever, charming photos and videos will garner you attention and followers. If you are a singer, you can include a snippet of a song (I would shy away from a full three-minute number.) If you are more of a dramatic actor, you might post a monologue. A strong caveat, though: only post your performing work if it is killer, if everyone raves about it. Show it to your friends; if their reactions are along the lines of "Good," "Nice," "I like it," trash that video. You only want to show superlative work. Otherwise, stick to the fun, amusing, relatable stuff.

Your smartphone can also serve as a recording device for self-submitted auditions. I sometimes use the Voice Memos app on my iPhone to send voiceover auditions as MP3 files. I also use my phone to record auditions for television and film. You don't need professional lights—just make sure the lighting you do have is bright enough to see your expression and relatively flattering. Buy an inexpensive, lightweight little tripod to keep your phone steady. Make sure you are loud enough (and if a friend is next to the camera feeding you lines, make sure they are not too loud—better they should be not quite as loud as you.) Frame yourself horizontally in a medium close-up (just above the head to mid-chest or just below the shoulders.)

Your Website

At some point, you will want to have a place where the world can find out about you and, more importantly, find out exactly what you want them to know about you. A personal website is a resource that you control and curate. It allows you to expand upon the bare bones of your professional résumé. It allows you to show almost unlimited alternatives to that one frozen image of you in your headshot. It allows you to express something of your personality and your creativity outside the limiting boxes of that standard headshot and résumé.

Actors' websites come in a bewildering array of styles and formats. There is no one right way to put one together. But there are a few basics. You want a website that is professional. Just as you would not send in a scratched photo mis-stapled to a juice-stained résumé, you don't want a confusing jumble of out-of-focus, unidentified production shots. You yourself can probably learn the rudiments of website design sufficiently to put up your first website, but unless you get really good, I would turn the reins over to a recommended website designer soon thereafter.

What do you want your website to do? You want it to be a sales tool to promote your career; you don't want it to be a scrapbook. You want it to tell the viewer/visitor right away who you are and what your experience has been—what you do and what you've done—and how to reach you to offer you an audition or a job. Do not make an agent or casting person do more than click on a single link to get that information. The first page of your website should have your headshot, a link to your résumé, a link to your video "reel," and an email address at which to contact you.

While you want your favorite headshot prominently displayed, you also have the opportunity to use some of your other headshots. You want production photos of your performances: in focus; interesting poses, sets and/or costumes; identified by your role, title of show, and where you did it; and if you worked with anyone famous/recognizable, preferably including a photo with him or her. If you have video on yourself—b-roll (publicity video) from stage productions, clips from television or film appearances—you will definitely want to feature that as well in a "Media" section. If you have positive newspaper, magazine, or Internet reviews of your work, you should include those in a "Press" section.

You might also include a timeline of your training and career. This is useful if you have some credits/experiences that don't lend themselves easily to a résumé format—such as workshops, industry readings, master classes, club acts/cabaret shows. If you have upcoming work, this is the perfect place to publicize such a fact in a "News" section. If you have a gap in your training/career of a year or so (or, God help us, more than one such gap), you might want to rethink the timeline.

You can include a biography that is more personal and (hopefully) charming than the usual playbill 50 to a 100 words. If you can write humorously, this is your chance. Funny is money. You will want a "Contact" section with your agent's contact information so that casting folks and directors know whom to call and, if you don't have an agent, with an email address (deadbeat@www.deadbeatactor.com) at which you can be reached.

In addition to your own website, your Internet presence can include a number of third-party sites. We have discussed the *Players Directory*, published by Now Casting, which features 125,000 actors, and which requires that you be a member of a professional union or signed by a SAG-franchised or ATA (Association of Talent Agents) member agency. If you are non-union or if you have completist tendencies, there is Actors Access.

Actors Access is free to join, as opposed to the $28 yearly fee for *Players Directory*. You create your own profile page with your headshot(s) and credits. You can upload up to two headshots for free; additional headshots are $10 apiece. Actors Access also offers something called a SlateShot, which is a Vine-length video (seven seconds) of you looking at the camera, showing a little personality, and saying your name. Using the same business model as your neighborhood drug dealer, Actors Access gives you the first SlateShot for free, and subsequent ones cost $5. You can upload a performance video and/or a demo reel for a cost of $22 per minute of video.

Actors Access also offers access to various auditions at a cost of $2 per audition. If you find yourself utilizing Actors Access to submit yourself for a lot of auditions, they offer a Showfax yearly membership for $68, which entitles you to unlimited free audition submissions as well as providing you with the "sides" (audition material) for the auditions. As an incentive to post a reel, actors who have a headshot, a résumé, a slate shot and a reel are higher up on the submission queue than those who just have the first three, who are higher than those who just have a headshot and résumé, and so forth. If you work through an agent, your Actors Access profile is what is used for electronic submissions, and if you haven't opened an AA account, the agent will open one for you from which to submit.

8

The Mental Climb

The Mindset of Success

Self-Esteem

Self-esteem is critical. You don't need to be the self-involved blowhard who is always telling people unasked about his latest triumph, but you do want to have that sense of "I'm the right person for this role" when you walk in to audition. Just as importantly, you want to have the sense that "I'm okay" and "I'm enough" when you're not auditioning, even when you haven't gotten an audition, let alone a job, in a while.

You—whoever you are—are not what you *do*. You are not what you *have*. You have value as a person whether you are starring on Broadway or lining up for a slot at an open call. Just as you wouldn't want success to go to your head and make you a total jerk, don't let lack of success define you either.

Lack of success can be debilitating, however. It is hard not to take on your lack of success as an identity: "I am a nonworking actor" or its existential variant: "I am an actor who does not act." There are two good ways to combat this.

One way is to act. Take what jobs—or nonpaying "jobs"—you can get. Keep busy. Work on your craft. Another way to work on your craft is by taking classes. Scene-study classes give you the chance to work on challenging material under a teacher's guidance. You get to do lots and lots of different roles. (I highly recommend pushing yourself—and your scene partners—to work every class or at every opportunity.) You get to stretch yourself with material you might not normally be cast in—some of those in the answer to question #4 of "The Four Questions" perhaps.

Create your own acting opportunities. Gather some friends in your living room for monthly or weekly play readings. Offer to be a reader for someone you know in the casting field. Write a scene or a minimovie and shoot it on your smart phone. Do it again. As well-known life coach Samuel Beckett says, "Try again. Fail again. Fail better."

If acting is not bringing you fulfillment in the way of cash and career, a second way is to do other things. I don't (necessarily) mean to do other things to make money. I'm talking about pursuing one of the other Five "C's," creativity—doing other things to fill your heart and your soul, to express and validate yourself. This could be some other creative, artistic endeavor such as painting or writing or jewelry making or weaving or photography or needlework. It could be a creative endeavor directly or tangentially connected to the Business: playwriting/screenwriting, directing, choreography, teaching voice or dance or acting, singing in a choir, headshot photography.

The truth is that even if you are successful as an actor, you are likely to have a lot of downtime. If you are in performance, that's only three hours a day (six on two-show days), leaving a lot of time at your disposal. And if you are doing television—or especially film—the name of the game is hurry up and wait. You will probably spend far more time in your dressing room or "three banger" trailer or hotel room than you will "on set." Reading, crossword puzzles, sudoku are all fine, but you might want to have some alternative creative endeavors in your back pocket.

Self-esteem is also to be found in another "C": community. Theatre is a second family, as I have said, and as you create your life in the Business, you will create your second family, your karass if you will. There is undeniable joy to be found in working together onstage for a common goal, and our joy is not confined to those moments when we are the stage-center focus of the enterprise. We feel fulfilled and we take pride in those moments when our cast-mates shine. It is a group endeavor. We are in this together.

That is true offstage as well. There is joy and pride and fulfillment to be found in helping your fellow "family" members, your karass-mates, with their careers and their lives. Alerting someone to an opportunity, walking their dogs, serving as an emergency babysitter, helping out with a move, being a sympathetic ear or a shoulder to cry on—all these kindnesses will bring you a sense of satisfaction at having been a friend, of having been useful, of having been of service.

Being useful, being of service is a powerful counteragent to the frustrations of the Business and the possibly inherent Fixation-on-Self that the Business can engender. One of my favorite quotes is this one by Rabindranath Tagore: "I slept and dreamt that Life was Joy. I woke and found that Life was Service. I acted and found that Service was Joy."

An inspirational minister and author named Forrest Church wrote that "Religion is our human response to the dual reality of being alive and having to die. Because we know that we are going to die, we question what life means. The purpose of our life is to live in such a way that our lives will prove worth dying for."

Without going overboard on community, I think that community and specifically service to your community is the key to a life worth dying for. I have had times in my life when I questioned whether acting was an appropriate or worthwhile thing to do with my life. I firmly believe that reflecting back to an audience truths and insights about themselves and their lives and their relationships is a worthwhile job. It is one of the reasons I so enjoyed telling the story of redemption in *Les Miz* all those years. If I had to defend my life to St. Peter, however, I would be more likely to draw upon examples of my service: my 20 years as a member of Equity's governing board, my five years as Equity president, my continuing service as a trustee of the Equity-League Pension and Health Funds, my mentoring of aspiring actors, and so forth.

I think we are here to make a difference. Although self-interest is one of our most powerful guiding forces, it is our contribution to others, the difference our lives make in the lives of others, that truly counts. We are social beings. We need community. and just as being interested in others is the surest way to be interesting, being useful to your community is the surest way to build a community that is useful to you.

And I encourage you not to play small. Expand your definition of community. Don't just be of service to your acting friends. Be of service to your apartment building, your church, your community board, your town council, your union, a soup kitchen, the Girl Scouts, Broadway Cares/Equity Fights AIDS, relief organizations, Habitat for Humanity, Actors and Artists Unite to End Alzheimer's (my friend Nancy Daly has turned her personal concern into this powerful and effective national fundraising network). Volunteer. Lift your eyes from your navel and focus on someone else's difficulties and concerns: your own concerns will seem less troublesome. Other people will appreciate you—not for your financial or acting success, but for your contribution to the community. You will appreciate yourself more. Even if you are all too often "an actor who doesn't act," you will be okay. You will be enough.

The last "C" is coverage—health insurance coverage. Coverage is hard to achieve in the acting biz. You can be a working actor by anyone's definition and still not work enough to get union-based health coverage. Equity requires 11 weeks of work in the past year to get 6 months of coverage; SAG-AFTRA requires 84 days of work or $18,000 in earnings during your base earnings period. So, you could work 10 weeks under Equity, make $15K in SAG-AFTRA, and be left with no coverage. The Affordable Care Act mandates that you be covered, so if (like most actors) you don't qualify for union health plan coverage, you need to look elsewhere. I recommend the Actors Fund of

America (www.actorsfund.org), which is an authorized advisor or "navigator" for healthcare coverage. Check out their Health Insurance Research Center and if you have questions, contact Renata Marinaro, National Director of Health Services (rmarinaro@actorsfund.org) for more information.

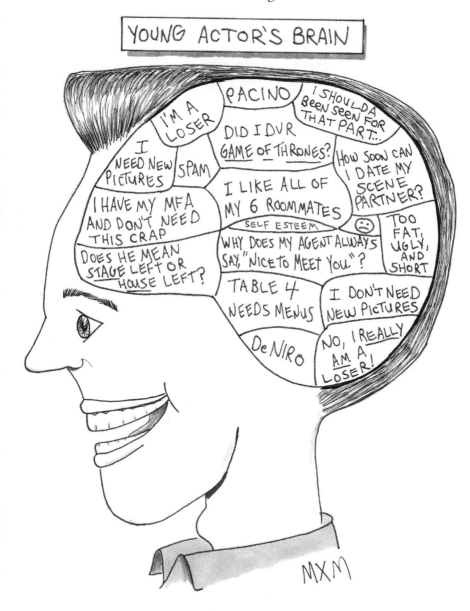

Tenacity

Among the keys that I have laid out to becoming a successful actor are attractiveness, skills (acting, singing, dancing), the ability to be funny, a pleasant personality, the ability to accept frequent rejection, and the persistence and tenacity to continue pursuing the profession. As I referenced early on in this volume, those last abilities—stick-to-it-iveness, if you will—generally trump talent in determining your success. An inability to handle rejection and a half-hearted approach to the Business will doom your career more surely than modest talent. To paraphrase *A Chorus Line*, I will bet on the person who is Drive:10/Act:3 over the one who is Act:10/Drive:3.

I draw your attention to the advice of that great actor Calvin Coolidge (not the most expressive of thespians and, given the Boston Police Strike, a little shaky in his union bona fides, but a highly successful man who knew when to get offstage): "Nothing in the world can take the place of persistence. Talent will not, nothing is more common than unsuccessful men with talent. Genius will not, unrewarded genius is almost a proverb. Education will not, the world is full of educated derelicts. Persistence and determination alone are omnipotent."

Sadly, though there are lots of acting schools and courses on acting, there are no tenacity schools and few courses on persistence and drive. (One possible coach you might check out is the wonderful Peter Pamela Rose and her—yes, she's a woman; her parents were just hedging their bets—Acting Business Boot Camp (www.actingbusinessbootcamp.com). Some people have this gift naturally—bravo for you if you are one of them—but I believe it can be developed as surely as acting skills.

The first thing to know is that most of the time the answer is going to be no. Accept that. Embrace that. Don't view every no as a damning indictment of your skills. An old salesman trick is to view every no as bringing you closer to a yes. If a salesperson made a sale to one out of every 20 prospects, he would put 20 pennies in one pocket and transfer one penny to his other pocket every time he made a call and got a no. With each no he could feel himself getting close to the yes.

Sales is a numbers game: the more calls you make, the more sales you are likely to make. Acting is not dissimilar: your success is dependent upon your opportunities, and your amount of opportunities has a lot to do with your amount of success. That is why people line up in the cold before dawn and why they are so keen to get an agent.

So yes, maximize your number of opportunities however you can, both because it will likely increase your chances of success and because it will remove some of the self-imposed tension and pressure on any one audition. And remember: you're not going to book every job you audition for. (Remember your old pal Sir Ralph Richardson's point that you can't do every job anyway because you can't take more than one train from the station.) Maybe you'll get 1 out of 20 or 1 out of 30. Enjoy the process and don't get monomaniacal about any one job.

As I said, back in the day when I carried around a Day Timer date book, I used to find it reassuring to glance back at the auditions I'd had five or six months earlier. Here were these musicals or TV shows or movies or plays that I had been obsessed with booking: almost without exception I had not booked them, and life had rolled on without a skipped beat. Looking at the various projects, I would easily remember how much I had wanted these jobs, but I had completely forgotten about them in the intervening months. No one job is the be-all and end-all.

So, between the utter unpredictability of casting folks and directors and the crazy odds against getting any one job, just relax and enjoy the process. Prepare for your audition thoroughly. Dress appropriately. Walk in with confidence. Be personable. Make strong choices. Be receptive to feedback and adjustments. Thank them with a smile and walk out with your head high. Then let it go. Do your best and let it go.

You can be fabulous in your audition and not get the job. That happens so often in the Business that it is a cliché. You may be, as I have related, too tall, you may be too short. You may not look enough like the previously cast person who is supposed to be your family member. You may look too much like some previously cast person. You may remind the director of his detested cousin. You may be perfect for the part, fabulous in the audition, and lose out because the director had already made up his mind to hire someone else. The powers that be could simply decide to "go another way." (This is the classic response when an agent or an actor inquires about an unsuccessful audition: "They went another way.") Imagine how those small, dark, unsmiling 35-year-olds felt when they saw how the director of *Die Hard* cast Matthias Targo.

Reviews, Critics, and Other People's Opinions

If you are anything like me, you want people to think you're wonderful—and to tell you so, repeatedly. If you are doing a show, and it is reviewed in the paper or on some Internet blog or website, you will want to read all the glowing things they have said about you. Don't do it.

Why not? you ask. There are many reasons. One, they may say less-than-glowing things about you. It is a truism about actors that if we get 19 wonderful reviews and 1 bad one, the bad one is all we remember. You don't need to go looking for things to undermine your confidence in your performance.

Secondly, they may say less-than-glowing things about the show you are doing, and you don't want to have your faith in your dramatic enterprise shaken. A bad review can make you question the worth of what you are doing, with unfortunate results for your performance. The reviews may say negative things about one or more of your fellow actors, and this plants in your mind the insidious seed of doubt about the abilities and merits of your fellows. Or the review may praise some other actor more than you, consequently breeding resentment. Even a review filled with praise can do damage: if a reviewer singles out as wonderful some moment or piece of business, it will inevitably make you self-conscious when you get to that moment.

There is no particular upside to reading reviews. You don't need another person's opinion of what you are doing; you just need your own instincts and the director's feedback. If you feel you must read what other people think of your show and your work, wait until your show closes.

The good news/bad news about a critic is that they see a lot of theatre. This gives them a vast repository of shows to which they can compare a particular production. That's the good news. The bad news is that seeing so many shows makes you jaded. A fun, pleasant show—that might be an ideal evening's entertainment for someone who sees a show or two a year—is dismissed as a trifle. An edgy, weird production that might well put off most theatregoers may be praised for breaking through the critic's ennui. And whatever merits critics and their judgment may have, part of their job is to sell newspapers or draw eyeballs to their sites. This can lead, in the name of "entertainment," to hurtful jokes at the actor's expense or callous remarks about an actor's physical appearance.

It has been said that a critic is someone who comes onto the battlefield after the battle is over and shoots the wounded. Brendan Behan famously described critics as "eunuchs in a harem: they know how it's done, they've seen it done every day, but they're unable to do it themselves." I am far less harsh on critics, especially those with the insight and perspicacity to have praised me, but I strongly advocate not putting your value and self-esteem in the hands of a stranger.

I would also advise not putting your value and self-esteem in the hands of a friend. As I said, the third eye you need is that of your director; don't add fourth or fifth eyes into the mix. Let your friends know that, in the words of Noel Coward, you love criticism just so long as it is unqualified praise. Seriously, a friend's remarks can be even more damaging than those of a critic. For some reason—perhaps so as not to appear as a soft touch or indiscriminately laudatory—friends seem to have a habit of tempering their enthusiasm for your work with a dig at one of your fellow castmates: "It was great, and I loved you! I wasn't so fond of the other guy." Let your friends know that you don't want to know what they think is wrong with the show or who they didn't like. Explain that this show is your family; and just as they wouldn't tell you that your mom is great, but your dad is sort of a jerk, you don't want them to tell you that your costar is kind of lame.

There is a corollary to this, and this is your responsibility. Remember my adjuration not to trash a show until you are at least two blocks away? Consider not trashing the show at all. If asked, you can say you're still thinking about it or that it wasn't really your cup of tea. You can choose to be kind instead of smart.

If you have a friend in the show and they know you are there, you have to go backstage or wait for them in the lobby. No excuses. Even if you hated the show. Wait for them or go back to see them and tell them they were great. That's it. Even if you thought they stunk. "You were great!" You can add things like, "Wow, what a show!" Or "I'm so glad I saw this." Or wherever your taste for elaboration and/or prevarication leads you. But tell them they were great. We all fear we are less-than-great, and we all want to believe that we are great. You will be doing your friends a kindness. Give them this gift.

If you feel that this is a shameful, dishonest way to live, if you feel that a true friend would tell a friend when he or she was not good or when his or her show was terrible, I completely understand. And I have an alternate career path for you. I suggest you become a critic.

How to Deal with Success

Doing a Long Run

Sometimes achieving success can actually be dispiriting because it is a human attribute to convince ourselves that we will be happy "when:" "when I get my own place," "when I have a boyfriend/husband/lover," "when I can buy a new car," "when I'm on Broadway," "when I get cast in a movie," "when I make $50K a year," "when I make $100K a year." Those stories we tell ourselves are convincing only so long as we don't achieve those goals. If Struggling Actress tells herself that she'll be happy once she is on Broadway making $100K a year, the reality of being on Broadway doing the same thing eight times a week for week after week may burst her bubble and send her in search of a new dream.

"Yay! My professional debut! Working with seasoned artists who are disciplined, passionate, and committed to their craft!"

Happiness doesn't come from success—any more than happiness comes from money or a new car or any other possession. Happiness comes from within. Bring happiness to your struggle, to your career; don't expect your career, whether it's a struggle or a cakewalk, to bring you to happiness. Enjoy what you do, and if you can't enjoy what you do, you should do something else. If auditioning makes you nauseated and the announcement of every show's cast fills you with bitterness and jealousy, maybe there's a better path for you.

The sad tale I posited of Struggling Actress, who achieves her dreams of Broadway and its attendant salary but finds that 400 performances per year of the same old same old is no fun, may well have had you rolling your eyes. It is my fervent hope that you, my reader, get to experience this predicament yourself. If you do, there are a couple of keys to making a long run a joy, not a trial.

I have done runs of over a year in five different shows, and I did two other shows over the course of multiple years on their tortuous road to Broadway. There is a world of difference in doing your high school or college production for two or four performances over a weekend or two and doing a show eight times a week for months and months on end. As my late friend and fellow *Phantom* castmate Richard Warren Pugh used to say, that's what makes it a craft, that's what makes it a job.

One can fall into a jaded insensitivity to one's show as the novelty wears off, and it can become frustrating to read on the theatrical websites about all your fellow actors doing new productions. Well, while they may (or may *not*) be accumulating credits in the creativity and career categories (thank you, Mrs. Davis), you are certainly outpacing them in the cash department.

I did *Les Misérables* on Broadway for over six years, and for 300 Fridays I would open the *New York Times* and read about some cool-sounding hopeful new production that I was *not* going to do. Almost every single one of those productions came and went, and I was still making a six-figure salary, building my pension, and putting my girls through college. I was also very fortunate to be doing a *wonderful* role in a *wonderful* show. My glass was certainly at least half full, but I *chose* to see it as brimming. Focusing on what you have rather than what you don't have: an attitude of gratitude is key.

Creativity is the other challenge. Adrenaline, inspiration, novelty, and the emotionality of performing for your folks will take you wherever you need to go for the student show you do for a couple Friday and Saturday nights. Five weeks into a professional run, there is no adrenalin, no inspiration, no parents, and you are wondering what the heck you ever saw or even pretended to see in the person playing opposite you. Then (or probably well before) is where craft needs to replace inspiration, where re-creation may replace creation.

Re-creation vs. creation is not an either/or, black/white duality. You don't want to slavishly recreate your performance night after night with the exact same intonation, the exact same gestures, and so forth. On the other hand, you don't want to reinvent the wheel every night with bizarre new choices that completely throw your scene partner and new blocking that befuddles (and perhaps endangers) your fellow actors and leaves the follow-spot operator either weeping or cursing. Somewhere in the middle between robotic sameness and disorienting unpredictability is best.

One of the many gifts of doing *Network* with Bryan Cranston was the opportunity to watch a master actor at work. Bryan as Howard Beale came up with brilliant, true, deeply human moments, but they were never exactly the same. He was consistent but ever new. He always seemed to be creating, never simply re-creating.

I will leave the necessary and useful exercises for this creative (or re-creative) craft to your acting teachers, but I will offer you a couple possibilities for regenerating a sense of novelty. A big source of novelty is the audience. No two audiences are the same; they are always a new scene partner. Are they whooping and hollering? Are they sitting on their hands? You will find that audiences on different days and different times have different personae. Tuesday and Thursday night audiences are there on a weeknight because they want to be there. Saturday night audiences are frequently too well fed and well liquored to be responsive and sometimes seem to be there at somebody else's suggestion or out of some keeping-up-with-the-Joneses cultural obligation. (The worst audience we ever had for *Phantom* was during our opening weeks when wildly enthusiastic crowds were the norm. It was a theatre party to support some ritzy Upper East Side private school, and these patrons had dutifully purchased tickets for huge sums of money to support the school. They spent the entire evening silently [*very* silently] congratulating themselves on their intellectual superiority to the entertainment on the stage of the Majestic.) Matinee ladies follow the plot like hawks—so if you have plot-based jokes, you're a golden girl (or guy). Every audience is different.

Speaking of audience novelty, one thing that fired my enthusiasm and gratitude during my six years in *Les Miz* was reminding myself that not only had most of the audience never seen *Les Miz* before, some of them had never been to a Broadway show. Some of them, indeed, had never seen a professional production before. I had the opportunity to *represent*, to fire up that patron with a lifelong enthusiasm for Broadway and professional theatre.

The silver lining to doing a long run is that you get two weeks of vacation a year. This is a double blessing in that not only do you get a break from the show, so do your fellow performers. And when the other performers are out, their understudy or the swing goes on—and the show is a little different! With two weeks of vacation per actor, any long-running show with a cast of 26 or more rarely has the exact same configuration 2 weeks in a row. On those rare occasions when we did not have anyone out on vacation or absent due to illness, the *Les Miz* stage managers would post on our call-board "FULL COMPANY TONIGHT!" in all caps. (I hear that *Mamma Mia* used to actually have a cake to celebrate these same very infrequent occasions.)

These are various ways to juice up your creativity within the show, but there are a number of ways to stay creative outside your performance. You can indulge your creativity in outside pursuits such as writing, photography, painting, and so forth, or in crafts such as woodworking, knitting, jewelry, beading, and the like. You can challenge yourself and keep your chops up with scene-study classes. You can do outside acting work such as readings/presentations/workshops of new shows, episodic TV, small film roles, or TV/radio commercials.

Plays Well With Others

My elementary school report cards had one side for academic skills and one side for social skills. One of the categories we were graded on was "Plays well with others." I don't recall receiving either exceptionally good (check-plus) or exceptionally bad (check-minus) grades in this area, but I strongly recommend that you aim for a check-plus.

My standard advice to young men about to get married is to tell them that they have one line in the script of their prospective marriage: "Yes, dear." Be agreeable. Be amenable. Validate your wife. Support her. I advocate being gracious and generally giving in to your spouse. Pick your battles and pick them judiciously. The same advice goes for an onstage partnership. When I launched into *Les Misérables*, I knew that most of my dramatic and comedic

REGINA REGRETS BEING ABSENT WHEN SCENE PARTNERS WERE ASSIGNED.

time would be shared with and dependent on Mme. Thenardier. I vowed to bring my best, most uxorious self to the relationship onstage and off. In my six years, I had three extraordinary women, three extraordinary comic actresses, three delightful partners: Fuschia Walker, Betsy Joslyn, and Aimee Garcia.

I tried to bring the classic improv mentality of "Yes, and . . ." to our rehearsals rather than one of "No" or "Okay, but . . ." Now, your author is not a shy lad, and he is bursting with comic ingenuity, but rather than following my standard approach of presorting all the ideas for our scenes into two categories: My Ideas and Not-as-Good Ideas, I would make it a point to try Fuschia's or Betsy's or Aimee's idea first. Sometimes, that was it—Bam! Winner! Sometimes, we'd go on to try my idea and that would work; frequently, we'd cobble together our approach with ideas from both of us and/or the directors. The important part for both my performance and our relationship was that I was amenable, I was open to suggestion. My acting teacher Wynn Handman used to say that good actors are "suggestible." This was doubly important each time the role was recast: I had to set aside my comfortable, proven-effective choices and open myself to what was new and different about my new stage-wife.

This produced wonderful relationships. I don't know whether it was because of my solicitousness onstage or because of her appreciation of my gifts as a Boggle player in our recurrent backstage games, but I can't count the number of times Betsy Joslyn would look up at me, smile, shake her head, and say, "You are such an asshole." (I would also like to state for the record that if the spline—the rubber cord that holds a screen in place on a window or door—breaks or wears out, obviously what you need to do is "respline," and that to question this word shows poor Boggle sportsmanship.)

Now despite my waxing theoretically rhapsodic about the unlooked-for delights of the swing/understudy going on and my breaking my arm patting myself on the back for my openness to new ways of doing things with Mme.

T, you should know that in practice I have been less delighted and open. I would get used to a certain way of doing things, to a particular way of creating the laughs with an intricate interplay of setups and payoffs. When an understudy Mme. T would go on (and I got the chance to work with at least four wonderfully gifted actresses who were Mme. T covers), I would tend to be Mr. Ingratitude, focused on every moment, look, bit, take, and piece of shared shtick that I wasn't getting rather than exulting in all the refreshing, interesting, different new things I was getting.

Among my most grievous faults—and I know you are astonished that Saint Nick has faults—is judgmentalism. Without my saying anything, and frequently without my being aware of what I am projecting, people feel that they are being mentally weighed in the balance and found wanting. (It is one of the reasons I am so frequently hired to play an Asshole in a Suit.) This unspoken judgmentalism was so strong the first night one of the Mme. T understudies went on that the woman actually burst into tears upon exiting the stage after our scene. So I need to take a healthy dose of my own advice. In the immortal words of Betsy Joslyn, "What an asshole."

Perspective and Comparisons

The Charlie Sheen/Donald Trump style obsession with winning, with being seen as a winner, can lead to a particular Show Business form of schadenfreude (a wonderful German word meaning "joy at another's misfortune"). To paraphrase Gore Vidal paraphrasing Somerset Maugham paraphrasing La Rochefoucauld: "It is not enough that one succeed; one must also have the failure of one's friends." I put it to you that in order to succeed, you don't need your friends to fail; you don't need anyone to fail.

In the flat world of near-instant social media mass communication, people rush to be the first to put the word out, to be seen as being in the know.

Sadly, the urge to be the first to trash somebody's stage or screen efforts seems to be stronger than the urge to be the first to champion someone. Do not give in to this. Building on the maxim of always waiting until you are two blocks away (or in your own car) before you say anything critical about someone's production, I encourage you to refrain from saying anything mean about other people's work, period. Instead, find what is praiseworthy.

I used to dichotomize people as either nice or smart. Nice people were generally not that smart, and smart people were frequently less than nice. For fear of looking like a sap and in an effort to demonstrate my refined sensibility and critical faculties, I have often joined in the head-shaking condescension and focused on the faults I have so cleverly found with some stage show. I encourage you to be a better person than I. Putting someone else down is a lousy and rather ineffective way of lifting yourself up—because life is not a zero-sum game.

It is up to you to determine your own success. And however much success you feel you have achieved on your path, on your journey up Rejection Mountain, it is only your path that counts. If you are anything like me, however, no matter how much you work, no matter how successful you have been, you can't help yourself from casting envious glances at those actors who "work all the time." I frequently find myself comparing myself to others—almost always those who *seem* to have more success than I do—and I have to continually remind myself that they are on a different path. It is like the Woody Allen joke: "I was thrown out of college for cheating on the metaphysics exam; I looked into the soul of the boy sitting next to me." Our job is to focus on our own path to the mountaintop.

Speaking of mountaintops, here are a couple of columns I wrote—both of them about the need for gratitude and perspective and one about a man who knew he had been to the mountaintop.

"You Have a Dream"

It was Martin Luther King Day recently, and while my fellow president was watching Beyoncé and James Taylor, I was talking and listening to our members in the newly established Albany, NY liaison area. Rev. King famously said, "I have a dream." You have a dream too. I am no oneiromantic (someone who divines by dreams), though I am clearly a pedant, but I believe you are living the dream.

When you were young, you dreamed of working in the professional theatre, of becoming a professional actor or stage manager. You have realized that dream. Perhaps your life may not seem so dreamy right now; your theatre work almost certainly doesn't pay all your bills, and it may be a very small part of the mosaic of your life. But you have achieved the distinction of being one of the tiny percentage of wannabe actors and stage managers to receive an Equity card.

I was profoundly moved by the actors I heard in Albany who admitted that they would probably be able to do more work if they were non-Equity, but they were still glad and proud to be Equity. I was equally moved while doing a reading last week to hear the tale of two actor friends who are raising a family in New Jersey. Despite their relative success (they have each been on Broadway), they are currently sinking into debt as they struggle to piece together a mosaic that will pay their bills.

We are the dreamers of dreams. In my acceptance speech for Equity's Tony Award last June (in which your pedantic president managed to misquote both Shakespeare and Yeats in the space of 30 seconds), I spoke of the centrality of dreams to our artistic lives. I love the quote I read recently of August Wilson, speaking to a young theatre director who was thinking of leaving the Business in order to make some money: "Your mom doesn't need you to buy her a house. She needs you to do the dreams she planted in you."

This is a maddeningly tough business, one whose default setting is no. In that same famous speech, Rev. King spoke of having been to "the mountaintop." If there were a mountaintop in the American theatre, it might well be Broadway, and I am lucky enough to have been there many times. Yet despite my unbelievable good fortune, I occasionally find myself in a seeming Slough of Despond, resentful and griping about the roles I didn't get and the yet-more-fortunate actors above me on our industry's peak.

When that happens, I remind myself of just how far up the mountain I am, and I remember to be grateful. You too, simply by having your Equity card, are on the upper slopes. Heck, just being an educated American gives you a leg up on the vast majority of people on this planet. So look down and say a little prayer of thanks. Then look up and keep climbing. You have a dream.

"Working All the Time"

"You work all the time." Perhaps you have said this to a fellow stage manager or actor. Perhaps people have said it to you. As a remarkably fortunate actor, I have heard it a lot; and for much of my career, it has been true—at least in the idiomatic "you always seem to be working" sense. But then, I have heard the phrase in recent months as well, and my Equity employment in the past three years has seemed to me all but nonexistent. Even counting my occasional forays into television, I wouldn't think I qualified as a man who is frequently—let alone constantly—employed.

I am not airing the dingy linen of my recent employment history in a bid for sympathy, but rather to illustrate two points. One, other people's careers always seem more glittering and successful than our own. This tendency to view our neighbor's grass as more verdant than our own has been exacerbated by the advent of the social media age. The tweets and Facebook posts touting someone's latest job, combined with the proliferation of theatre-oriented websites with their stories about other people's readings, development projects, and workshops (as well as actual productions) can make one feel relatively unemployed if not unemployable.

But this reflects the inherent bias of the reporting. Most of our career efforts are not newsworthy or even Facebook-worthy. Being typed out at the Equity Chorus Call, receiving an overly sincere "Thanks for coming in!" at your audition, going five weeks between auditions, not hearing back after dropping off your stage management résumé, blowing the callback for the job you wanted—these stories don't show up on the Internet, but they greatly outnumber the stories of triumph and success.

Which brings me to point two: nobody works all the time. Very few people even work most of the time. No matter how successful our career looks to our neighbor, we all go through the same anxieties when a show closes without another job lined up. We all fret over jobs we can't get seen for, over auditions we screwed up ("I should have done it this way!"), over upcoming bills. As I have written before, we all put together pieces to form the mosaic of our working lives, and if we're lucky, many of the pieces are acting or stage-managing jobs. But that luck or the lack of it doesn't determine if we are a professional stage manager or actor: that question is answered by the plastic card in our wallet.

I recently ran into an actor who reminded me of our meeting 18 months ago. He had come to New York as a last-minute replacement for the local liaison to represent his liaison city at an all-day gathering of the 27 chairs of the local liaison committees; and by the afternoon, he was moved to a confession. He didn't feel right, he wasn't sure he should be representing his city, he didn't even feel like an actor: he hadn't acted in 3 years. I was quick to assure him that he was as much an actor as anybody in the room, that everybody went through dry patches—whether it was a couple of weeks or a couple of years. He was a full-fledged, card-carrying member.

We each have our own particular path in life, and our job is to do the best we can on that path. Comparing our path to someone else's is a fool's game, particularly if the other path belongs to Tom Hanks, Anne Hathaway, Danny Burstein, or Laura Osnes. In the course of any one year, only about one-third of our membership gets *any* sort of Equity job. Think about that next time you're beating yourself up for your employment record. And the other two-thirds? Some of them may have temporarily stepped aside from the pursuit of Equity work, but the rest are working: preparing material, auditioning, doing scene study, taking voice lessons, taking dance classes, making connections, scouring *Casting Call* for possible jobs. I always say that my real work is looking for work—the job is merely the reward. So actually, I *am* working all the time. And probably, so are you. Let's keep working, each on our own career path.

"Three years on a sitcom, now my first play!
I'm finally getting the respect I deserve."

9

Choosing, Changing, Creating Your Path

The Power of No

The Work You Want to Do vs. the Path of Least Resistance

Being an actor is a life spent, for the most part, hoping to be chosen. There isn't a lot of power or choice or agency in that. You may well never get to the rarefied heights of an "offer only" actor who picks and chooses from the projects proffered to her or him, but you don't have to passively drift through your life waiting to be asked.

Do what you can to create the work you want to do: jobs that will reward you creatively and financially, jobs that will bring you satisfaction, fulfillment, and forward momentum in your career. Do your research. Find out as well as you can what projects and productions are in process. Figure out which of those have roles that will move you forward in your craft or your career. Do whatever you can to get yourself seen for those roles.

At a certain point, you will get some traction in the Business. You will be seen. You will get work. You will get some more work. And opportunities will begin to open up to you. These opportunities initially are likely to be for work that is More of the Same—because there are a superabundance of actors and, as I have said, casting directors necessarily resort to pigeon-holing and categorizing to save their sanity. Be careful how far down this path of least resistance you go. You want to keep your eye on the prize, the prize of the work you want to do.

If you've broken through as a musical comedy performer, it will be easier to get another musical comedy job. If you've done a half dozen musicals in a row, however, you will be known and thought of as a musical comedy performer, and it may be more difficult to get seen for that straight play. Similarly, if you are a triple threat and you parlay your breakthrough job singing and dancing in the chorus of a Broadway show into two or three more chorus jobs, you may find yourself labeled a chorus performer and find it difficult to get auditions for featured or leading roles. People who've demonstrated that they have the skills of a standby (nonperforming understudy for a leading role) or a swing (singer-dancer who covers every male or female track in the ensemble) may find themselves much sought after for these jobs, but often only for these jobs.

After I'd gotten my first Equity job (a musical), my next job was two musicals at Goodspeed Opera House, one of which came to Broadway. That musical, *Very Good Eddie*, got me established in the Business and brought me agents for both legit work and for commercials. A couple of months after *Eddie* closed, I accepted a job standing by for two roles in *The Magic Show*. The job paid me Broadway money, and it kept me in town so I could audition for other things, but it was in no sense a step forward in my career. It was another musical (one I wasn't even performing in), and at the time I was probably making more money from TV commercials than I was from *The Magic Show*.

After a year or so, I decided to jump ship; but when I was cast in a classy production of a straight play—Eugene O'Neill at the Long Wharf—I couldn't get out of my contract in time to do the show. Later that year, I managed to escape *The Magic Show* and do two straight plays at two different regional theatres, and I think I took some of the "only does musicals" stigma off myself. I have returned to regional theatres selectively since then, choosing jobs that feed me creatively in exchange for not being in town and available for higher-paying, higher-profile work. Regional theatre work can be wonderful creative work, and it can also be a way to counter-balance a preponderance of musical credits. It is, however, work that will keep you afloat financially but will not fatten your savings account. Your work will also not be seen by the powers that cast television and film, so its value to your career is to pad your résumé and hope that impresses some future casting director. Be careful how far down this path you go.

Why *Not* to Do a Job

The biggest milestone in an actor's career is often getting that first professional job. I posit that perhaps the second biggest milestone is the first time an actor turns down a job. The Business and the common wisdom thereof relentlessly drum into our consciousness that jobs are scarce as hens' teeth. The prevailing attitude is supposed to be: "I am lucky to be working." "I should be grateful for this job."

I am a big fan of gratitude, but sometimes the appropriate response is "Thanks but no thanks." Saying no is a powerful antidote to the general feeling of powerlessness that the Business can inculcate. Once you have said no to a job, you have broken the shibboleth that you have to take whatever crumbs fall off the Table of Life. You are no longer at the effect of life, you have some say in the matter. You are in a sense no longer in the line hoping for some government cheese, you have jumped to the local market where you get to shop, to actually *choose* your food.

Of course, if you are anything like me, you will feel guilty for saying no. I want everyone to like me, and I hate to disappoint people. Well, when you turn down their show, people inevitably are disappointed. They may even dislike you, at least temporarily. So you'll want to feel as secure as you can in your own reasoning for saying no.

I have recently said no to several opportunities, and while I had good reasons, I still felt guilty. One show I had actually auditioned for and agreed to do(!); the others were unsolicited offers. The show I had agreed to do was a fun role in a classic musical at two regional theatres—one of them 3,000 miles away. Ten days before rehearsals were to start for the musical, the Long Wharf Theatre called me to see if I would join the cast of the world premiere of Joe DiPietro's play *The Second Mrs. Wilson*, which was beginning rehearsals in two days (an actor had had to drop out). I read the script and talked with my wife and my agent. New play vs. old musical and driving distance vs. 3,000 miles away made it a clear-cut decision: I jumped ship. I made it a point to write a heartfelt personal letter of apology to the director of the musical.

Of the other opportunities, one conflicted with my recovery from some foot surgery, one was just less money than I wanted to work for, and one was for a play that I found distasteful in its licentiousness and violence. Getting another, better opportunity is always the best reason to turn down work, though I can assure you from personal experience that the director of the turned-down show always sees his own particular show as the better opportunity—no matter what a dispassionate observer might opine.

Prince of Broadway

I actually jumped ship on Hal Prince three different times. I first encountered Hal in early 1974 when, after taking an audition class with his casting director Joanna Merlin, I auditioned for Count Carl-Magnus in the national tour of *A Little Night Music*. Like the guy in *The Producers* who auditioned for the gypsy lover, I didn't get it. Four years later, I came down from Hartford where I was doing a play to audition for a new Stephen Sondheim musical called *Sweeney Todd*. They liked me and brought me back to the final callbacks for not one, but three, different roles: Antony, Tobias, and the Beadle. I didn't get it. I didn't get it. I didn't get it. Even though I went 0 for 3, Joanna evidently leaned over to Hal and, pointing to me, said, "When Kevin leaves . . ."

Kevin was Kevin Kline, who had recently won a very well-deserved Tony Award for playing Bruce "Boo-Boo" Granit in *On the Twentieth Century* and whose contract was in renegotiation. Kevin re-signed but gave his notice that fall to do Michael Weller's *Loose Ends* down at the Arena. From Pittsburgh where, as Lennie in *Of Mice and Men*, I was busily breaking my future wife's neck eight times a week, I flew back to audition for Bruce Granit, and they offered me the role.

Now—I already *had* a job. I had been working on scenes from *Ethan Frome* in my Wynn Handman scene study class that summer, and the woman playing Zenobia and I had talked William Esper into directing us in an Off-Broadway production at the WPA Theatre on 23rd Street after I got back from Pittsburgh. So . . . Ethan Frome or Bruce Granit. My agents were practically apoplectic that I would even consider turning down this high-profile Broadway job (and its attendant salary) for some no-name Off-Broadway revival. I chose *Twentieth Century*—not for the money and not even for the opportunity to work with Hal Prince et al. It was mainly because after 10 weeks of living with the inarticulate, struggling, tragic character of Lennie Small, I was reluctant to segue immediately into another few months of an inarticulate, struggling, tragic character. Give me the fun musical. (I don't think Bill Esper ever forgave me.)

I joined the merry gang at the St. James Theatre. Paraphrasing the tagline for that year's *Jaws 2*, I posted on the callboard: "Boo-Boo 2—Just When You Thought It Was Safe to Get Back on the Train." I did the last 10 or 11 weeks of the run, then took my new girlfriend/future wife to Barbados for a vacation. While in Barbados—pre-email, pre-fax-machine Barbados—I got a couple of phone calls from my agent. One was to audition when I returned to be Jill Clayburgh's boyfriend in a new movie, and the other was to relay Hal's fervent wish that I play Bruce Granit in the national tour of *On the Twentieth Century*.

I was making good money doing television commercials, and I had no wish to abandon my new girlfriend to travel around the country in the company of Rock Hudson and Judy Kaye, particularly since they had already agreed to allow Kevin to play Bruce Granit when the show was sitting down in LA. So I said no. Sorry, Hal. The role went to a wonderfully funny and talented actor named Patrick Quinn, who was one of my predecessors as Equity president. Kevin's production of *Loose Ends* came to Broadway, so he did _not_ do the show in LA. Patrick was a big success in LA and got a five-figure development deal with ABC-TV. So it goes.

(Oh, the Jill Clayburgh movie? The character was the boyfriend she leaves to take up with Michael Douglas. It was my first significant movie audition, maybe my first movie audition period, and I worked like a demon on the sides—I guess they were express mailed to me or something. When I got back, I went in to read for director Claudia Weill and Jill Clayburgh. They were delightful, but when we began to read, we weren't connecting at all: I had the wrong sides. They must have sent me old sides or something. It was a mess. I don't know why they didn't copy the new sides for me and send me out for 10 minutes to work on them. I must not have been close enough to what they were looking for. They told my agents later, "Who would leave him for Michael Douglas?" I doubt that was truly their reasoning, but it eased the pain a bit.)

Fast forward eight years and *The Phantom of the Opera* is coming to Broadway, riding a tsunami of publicity and rave reviews. The three leads in London—Michael Crawford, Sarah Brightman, and Steve Barton—are coming over with the show. The next best roles are Carlotta, the prima donna of the Paris Opera; and the two managers of the Opera, Firmin and André. The gracious André likes opera while the grumpy Firmin likes only money. They both have fairly wide baritone ranges, but apart from that, there are few limitations on who might play the role. The roles have been played by men in their 30s and men in their 70s.

We were asked to sing an operatic aria for our first audition. (I did "Eri Tu" from *Un Ballo en Maschera*.) I must have been acceptable, because I was called back and told to prepare the managers' scene, including the song "Prima Donna," from act 1 of *Phantom*. At the time, I was rehearsing the workshop of Peter Allen's *Legs Diamond*, and our wonderful rehearsal pianist Tim Stella worked on the song with me.

For the callback, a couple dozen of us—glorious voices, hundreds of Broadway credits—are brought to the Royale Theatre (now the Jacobs) and are stacked up backstage left as Hal, Andrew Lloyd Weber, Gillian Lynne, and boy-wonder musical director David Caddick listen to us all and then begin the process of mixing and matching. I am in a good mood, happy to see Hal, who seems happy to see me, and I have a grand time with the songs. Deciding that Firmin is the older, wiser alpha dog of the partnership, I belittle the world of opera and belittle André's concerns. When Carlotta threatens to pull out of the production, I am disgusted and exasperated, but knowing what side my financial bread is buttered on, I pull out all the stops to bring her back: imploring, kneeling as I plead, pulling André down to kneel beside me. I get some laughs. I do it with one potential André, then go offstage and wait while another pair sing. I do it with another André, then another. Soon it becomes clear that the mixing and matching has come down to Who Fits Best with Wyman. I go home in a state of cautious euphoria, and indeed the offer—an outrageously lowball offer courtesy of my favorite frugal Scotsman Cameron Mackintosh—comes in a few days later.

After I had been doing *Phantom* for a year and concerned by a vision of a future that had me as Firmin for the next 10 years (I could not then conceive that the show would still be running 30 years later), I was offered the role of

Ken Howard's replacement in the latest Neil Simon play, *Rumors*. I gave my notice to *Phantom* and then had to go crawling back to our general manager when Manny Azenberg, the producer of *Rumors*, decided he needed a bigger name to boost the box office, hired Larry Linville from *M.A.S.H.*, and rescinded my offer. I don't think Hal and Cameron were pleased that I seemed to be so eager to bail on their megahit. Sorry, Hal.

Five years later, I was back working for Hal—and in the process, probably setting some sort of Equity record by being paid on three separate contracts at once. I was performing at night in a new Off-Off-Broadway musical called *Brimstone*, and for Hal I was workshopping during the day a new Michael John La Chiusa musical at the Public Theatre called *The Petrified Prince*. I had also accepted a position as standby for Higgins and Pickering in that year's Broadway revival of *My Fair Lady*—and *Brimstone* understood that if *MFL* called, I would not be doing *Brimstone*.

The Petrified Prince was zany and lots of fun. I was the Pope, and my cardinal Tim Jerome and I were lovers. The Public decided to mount a full production in the '94–'95 season, but by that time I was channeling my inner small, dark, unsmiling 35-year-old for *Die Hard*. So I had to say no. Sorry, Hal. Maybe the third time was the charm, because I never worked for Hal again.

The Five Insufficient "C's" (C What I Did There?)

Those Five *C*'s of why to take a job are also a good source of reasons why not to take a job. Lack of cash is a key one—if it's not going to pay you enough, it may well be a nonstarter. Lack of creativity: I have actually turned down a couple of Broadway shows because the role, the track didn't interest me sufficiently (it helped that these were back in the days when I was making good money doing TV commercials.) Career: I have turned down the opportunity to do shows I have already done before, and I have turned down the opportunity to do shows in venues far from the eyes of those who might cast me in the next career-advancing role.

For years, indeed, I was loath to take roles in regional theatres or to do a national tour—not so much because casting agents were unlikely to see me as because I was unlikely to see my wife and kids. Early on in our relationship, my wife was cast in three separate regional theatre productions in the space of several months. She turned them all down because she didn't wish to risk our relatively new relationship by going out of town for a couple months. Some years later, I turned down George in ACT's *Sunday in the Park* for similar reasons.

Our acting careers are important, but they are probably only part of what we do for a living. And what we do for a living is only part of our life. Family, friends, a significant other may well take precedence over a job. When we lose out on a job, we can remind ourselves that acting work is not the be-all and end-all of life. It is also not the be-all and end-all of life when we get the job. We need balance in our lives.

The appropriate time, the best time to make those decisions, is before you audition for the role, not after you have been offered the job. It is very frustrating and profoundly irritating to a director and/or a casting person after they have gone through the agonizing process of assembling the jigsaw puzzle that is a show's cast to have their carefully chosen actor say, cavalierly, "Oh, no, I don't want to do that," without a really good excuse. Frequently even a really good excuse doesn't do much to ease the frustration and irritation. My wife was never cast again at any of those three regional theatres, and I have never worked at ACT. So never audition for a job you don't intend to take; it is rude and unprofessional. The idea that even though you wouldn't accept an offered job, it will be good just to be seen and show your skills off is self-centered thoughtlessness.

Now in my wife's defense, she auditioned for all three shows in good faith; it was just that, faced each time with the concrete reality of ten weeks apart from her new serious boyfriend, she demurred. Stuff happens. You get another job offer. Someone gets sick. A new relationship blooms. It is not a crime to turn down a job—but if you auditioned for that job, I strongly advise you to write a sincere and personal letter of apology and appreciation to the director (and if you're wise, the casting director).

Creating Your Path

Taking the Long View/Visualization

If you want a career, a decades-long career in the Business, you want to focus on the big picture. You want to take the long view. That long view should be a prospective vision. You want to focus on where you want to be, and then consider whether you are on the right path.

Where do you want to be in one year? In five years? In ten years? In twenty years? In six months? How about in one month? Where do you want to be geographically? NY? LA? City? Country? Suburbs? Are you living in a house? An apartment? Houseboat? Are you living with roommates? A spouse? Kids? Pets? What sort of acting are you doing? If your acting isn't your only source of income, what else are you doing to make money? What else are you doing with your time and energy, even if it doesn't make money? (Making jewelry? Decoupage? Teaching Sunday School? Helping out at a shelter? Sponsoring people in a twelve-step program?)

You can start with your ten-year vision/plan or your one-year vision/plan or even your one-month vision, depending on how comfortable you feel with projecting your future. If you don't have a strong preference, start with your farthest projection—twenty years. See your future self. Where are you living? How big is this place? What does it look like? Be specific. With whom are you sharing your domicile? If you have a car, what make and model is it? See the work you are doing and with whom you are doing it. Since this is an exercise to support your acting career, be as specific about this portion as you possibly can—in terms of places you are working, material you are working on, people you are working with, the amount of money you are making.

Once you have your twenty-year vision clear in your mind, put it down on paper. Write it all down. Now you know where you want to be. This is the mountaintop you are heading toward. Now how are you going to get there? Start working backwards with your vision. Ten years, five years, one year, six months, one month. See if you can't create a series of visions that support the next vision and build on the previous one. As you get closer to the present day you, your visions will bear more relationship to your current situation and should seem more easily attainable.

Once you have your visions written down, take a look at your one-month vision. What concrete steps do you have to take to achieve that? What steps might you take to bring that vision about? What do you need to do? Who do you need to be? Start being that person. Start doing those things. Take the first step. Take the next right step. Keep going.

Progress is not a straight line. Setbacks are not fatal. Remember: most of your auditions yield a job for somebody else. That's okay. Keep going. Every once in a while, lift your head up from the daily struggle and look at the mountaintop—in other words, consult your twenty-year plan. Are you heading in the right direction? Are you on your way to that twenty-years-older you?

For most of us, the mountaintop stays pretty much the same—we just find ourselves wandering rather aimlessly around the foothills. That what this exercise can do for you—it can remind you where you want to be, where you should be heading, and give you some impetus to put yourself back on the right track.

Your plans can change. You may realize that you don't want to be doing a sitcom and living in Encino, that you want to be a member of the Oregon

Shakespeare Festival and living outside Ashland. (Or vice versa.) Or you may realize that you want to be a director and that your twenty-year plan is to be the artistic director of Trinity Rep. Or you may discover that your greatest joy is not acting but writing and illustrating children's books. Or it is teaching kids in a Montessori school. Or running a dance studio. Or teaching voice. That's fine. Redo all your visions because you have a new mountaintop.

Stick-to-it-iveness and persistence do not mean rigid inflexibility. Keep going, keep attacking your career, keep working toward your Acting Mountaintop—as long as that is what you want. At some point, you may realize that you don't want the struggle, that indeed even if the struggle went away, you would no longer want the goal you were struggling for. That's okay. That's one of the reasons to keep checking with yourself as well as checking on that mountaintop.

Other Sources of Strength, Stability, and Self-Esteem

Let's assume that you are clear that your particular mountaintop is about acting. That's great. As I have maintained previously, I judge potential jobs on how well they satisfy the Five *C*'s: Cash, Career, Creative, Coverage and Community. I hope your acting work regularly ticks all five boxes. For most folks, however, simply getting work of any sort can be frustratingly difficult. As you seek a career in this business and work that fulfills that particular *C*, let's examine some alternative sources of those other *C*'s.

Cash: Cash is king. You need money to live, so if it is not coming from acting work, you need another source: a day job, as we have discussed previously. But as you look for ways to bring more money in, focus equal attention on ways to reduce the amount of money flowing out. Shrink your financial footprint. Ask yourself before a financial outlay, Is this something I *need* or something I *want*? Live simply. Don't be a suffering martyr of abnegation, but don't fall into the habit of rewarding yourself (or consoling yourself) by spending money. Remember: a rich person is someone who makes $50K and spends $48K; a poor person is someone who makes $50K and spends $52K.

Set aside money for savings. A prudent amount is three months' worth of expenses. Pay yourself first, say the experts. In other words, don't pay all your bills and buy all the things you want and *then* see if you have some money left to put into savings. This latter plan is the classic Nick Wyman method, which yielded exactly *zero* money for savings most years. I would convince myself that I *deserved* the material possession, the trip, the meal, and so forth, and I clinched the deal by reminding myself of my plan to make even more money the following month or the following year. And if I *did* make more money? I spent it. So don't be like me. Don't do as I did; do as I say.

Pay yourself a percentage of every paycheck (5 percent? 2 percent? 10 percent?) Or pay yourself a set amount when you pay your rent and your other fixed bills. Keep doing this and the money will grow into your three-month cushion. Don't stop there. Keep doing it, and you will have the ability to do all sorts of remarkable things, from choosing to do an acting job for reasons other than money to buying a place to live.

Creative: Exercising our creativity onstage or onscreen is probably the number one reason why people chose to go into this nutty business. Experiencing the inner life and the emotions of a character was a rewarding challenge. Experiencing the laughter and applause of an audience was a rush. Performing was a delicious, filling feast. Unfortunately, acting as a professional, it can be a long time between meals, and sometime the meals are less than satisfying.

To counter this, when you have the opportunity to perform you should generally take it. (There are exceptions to this, as I discussed in "The Power of No.") I am a big fan of experiencing actual performing on a stage as the best way to learn how to act. Acting regularly prevents you from getting rusty, enables you to keep up your chops. It is a way to move forward in your skills as well as to avoid slipping backwards.

It is preferable to work regularly, not only for maintaining your skills but also for maintaining your sense of yourself as a working actor. A powerful reason to accept work is the psychological one of having an answer to the questions "Are you doing anything?" or "What have you been doing?" The answer to the first is all too often "No" or "Nothing," and if the answer to the second is a project you did six months or a year ago, you can easily feel like a nonparticipant in the Business of Show.

As I get farther and farther from my last job, my standards of pay and prestige get lower and lower. A stretch of unemployment definitely whets my appetite for that job possibility out of town or that low-paying festival show in town. When I am working, I can be pretty picky. I did the original staged reading presentation of *The Producers* with Nathan Lane, Gary Beach, Cady Huffman, et al., but I was happily ensconced in *Les Miz*, which seemed like a surer bet. When John Dossett took a leave of absence from *Newsies* to do Michael John La Chiusa's *Giant* at the Public, I turned down the audition to replace him because I had been cast in a new Broadway show: *Rebecca*. Well, *The Producers* outran *Les Miz*, and *Rebecca* never made it into rehearsal. (I don't always make the right decisions.)

"That's my grandson! Third on the left! With the blue shirt, the brown hair, and the abandoned medical career!"

Changing Your Path

Why Am I Here?

"Why am I here?" has a certain philosophical, practically spiritual aspect to it—and that makes it an even more useful question. Yes, you want a job; yes, you want money; yes, you want applause and recognition; but I have a suspicion you may ultimately want something else more. I think you want to be useful, to make a difference in the world, to be of service and to be part of a loving connection with others. (Of course this is what I want, so perhaps I am projecting. Perhaps.)

When we are acting in a play that is hitting on all cylinders, we feel useful to the enterprise, of service to the director and our fellow actors, that we are making a difference in the world, and we absolutely feel part of a loving connection with others. When we are acting in a turkey, we can still feel that we are useful and of service and we often still feel part of a loving connection with others; as for making a difference in the world—well, that may be too much to hope for.

"Part of a loving connection with others." I think we want that more than money, more than applause. We want to have a loving relationship with an individual who loves us completely despite our myriad flaws. We want to have a family. That might be our family of origin, it might be a family we create with a spouse and children, it might be a family of like-minded souls who do theatre together—or fly-fishing or knitting or a 12-step program. We are social creatures who crave connection, and theatre is a wonderful way to create that. Each show creates a family. Theatre has enabled me to experience being a part of dozens and dozens of families. I started out as the kid and rapidly morphed into the dad. I have had a few surrogate parents, several surrogate brothers, and lots and lots of surrogate children. I didn't start out looking for new families or even a new family; but looking back I think that's at least part of what I was seeking and may be why I am here.

What Else Might I Do?

Whether you are striding along a clear path to the Mountaintop of "Successful Acting Person" or you are lost in the weeds of frustration, you will need to pay your rent and buy food. You will probably need a "day job," and you may well decide at some point that you need a "different job." What else might you do? What skills and qualifications do you have?

You may not have an MBA, but you have a lot to offer a prospective employer. A trained actor is:

*creative

*a good communicator

*able to take direction

*flexible

*a team player

*a people person

At the beginning of your career, and quite possibly throughout most or all of it, you will need to do something besides acting to make enough money to pay your bills. First of all, know that that is okay—that it doesn't make you not a professional actor or less of an actor: it's just what's so about the Business.

As I indicated earlier, a job should give you the flexibility to audition for work and, ideally if you get acting work, rehearse and perform without having to give up the job. Waitressing, bartending, proofreading, temping, teaching voice, driving a cab or an Uber/Lyft/Get car, real estate agent, Starbucks barista, website designer are all common choices for "day jobs." Some of these—website designer, Uber driver, Starbucks barista—didn't exist 35 years ago. Some—teaching dance or voice or acting, designing websites—may develop into a second career or a new mountaintop.

Flexibility and enough money to pay your bills, and—preferably—something you enjoy doing. If you *hate* your day job, it is not going to do good things for you or your life (and probably your acting) no matter how remunerative it might be. If you really like your day job, it might turn into your career.

Another Mountaintop

At some point, you may decide that you no longer want to go to the Mountaintop of "Successful Acting Person": the weeds of frustration are too much or your path is too rocky or too steep or too long or any one of a dozen other reasons. If that happens, you will certainly not lack for company.

I know lots and lots of actors who have left the Business to do something else. That's one of the ways the Business handles the excess of actors. It's as if the Business were this airline that overbooks all its actor flights knowing many will cancel or not show up. And it is not entirely lack of success that causes folks to drop out. Some very successful friends of mine have left the Business. For whatever reason, the appeal was gone—they were no longer willing to engage in the battle.

Lack of success, however, is still the biggest reason for leaving the profession: lack of quality opportunities to act and lack of financial remuneration. There are far more actors than acting jobs, so it's hard to get even low-paying acting work. At a certain point, an actor may say, "Why am I continuing to try to be a professional actor? I never get the chance to act." This is an understandable response to the overwhelming difficulty of the Business, and that actor may well decide to leave the Business.

Another actor may have sufficient opportunities but find herself working three low-end, no-future jobs just to have enough money for rent and food. Clearly someone who chooses to be an actor is not driven by money, but we all need to pay the bills. Most actors could make more money doing something else. (Although I am a successful actor, I could have made far more money had I followed my classmates into investment banking or corporate law.)

The way the Business works is that thousands and thousands of aspiring actors in their early 20s flood NYC and LA. Living in poverty or semipoverty with legions of their fellow struggling artists, they scuffle through their 20s into their 30s doing odd jobs, finding occasional employment as actors, cycling through short-term relationships, occasionally relying on the generosity of their parents, sharing a fifth-floor walkup with two friends. At a certain point in their 30s, however, these aspiring actors reevaluate their lives—particularly in comparison with their high school and college friends. These friends have well-paying jobs, houses, cars, spouses, kids: they are adult, firmly settled in their careers and on their way to their own mountaintop. In the face of such comparisons (and remember, I do not recommend comparing your path to anyone else's), it can be hard to justify your continued struggle to succeed as an actor.

So it is true that most actors do not succeed in making a living solely as an actor. It is also true that many, perhaps most, aspiring actors eventually turn away from acting and choose to do something else. Choosing to do something else is perfectly rational and may make perfect sense for you. There are many jobs that keep you in (or very near) the Business: agent, casting person, voice teacher, accompanist, dance teacher, dresser, Equity business rep, acting teacher. Your experience will stand you in good stead with all those career paths.

If you love the Business and the Business isn't loving you back, consider a slightly different relationship. Or you may decide that you want or even demand a job that offers you money, security, career advancement, and so forth. Great. Go for it. Don't do it because you don't like the way your life looks in comparison with someone else's. Do it because you have a new mountaintop you want to aim for. But if you still have the same acting mountaintop, keep going. Review this book and its suggestions. Keep what's working. Drop what isn't working and try a different tack.

To succeed as an actor, keep studying, keep challenging yourself with the jobs you take or the scenes you choose in class. Stay connected with people. Use the connections you have. With delicacy and appreciative acknowledgement, leverage those connections to get job opportunities. Make new connections. With all your connections, give more than you get.

Give more than you get. It works in life; it works onstage. Listening, focus, and attention are great tools onstage: they seem like something you do for the other actor, but it actually benefits you just as much. I like to think of myself as being great with text (give me that endlessly pontificating Shavian role, that fabulous four-minute Paddy Chayefsky monologue), and I love to be the center of attention, the star (thank you, LBJ in *All the Way*), but I have generally been better when my character has little to say and a strong need to listen to and focus on others.

Bring that listening, focus, and attention on others into your daily life. It will win you more friends and influence more people than any anecdotes or life-of-the-party antics. As I said before, be interested, not interesting. We actors, despite our dazzling good looks, effortless charm, and displays of confidence, are riven by the thought that we are not okay, that we are not enough. We are needy, insecure people, and sadly, success will not cure that disease. The answer to that neediness and insecurity is not bigger, more important roles or more money: it is feeling useful, feeling a loving connection to others, being of service. So as you launch yourself into the pursuit of acting work, know that your self-worth and self-esteem do not depend on your success or lack thereof. It depends more on your contribution to the world, on your being useful, on your being of service.

Find opportunities for service. You don't need to have piles of cash to contribute. You probably have time to contribute, and as those of us in the latter third of our lives can tell you, time is far more valuable than money. Frequently, people tell themselves that they will contribute to a charitable organization at some future time when they have more money; sometimes that day of perceived financial sufficiency never comes—not because the money doesn't come but because the people still fear they don't have enough. Sometimes people don't participate in service or contribute to others because they feel that they don't have enough time, that they need to work on themselves, that they are not sufficiently okay. Don't buy into this. I am here to tell you, my fellow needy, insecure actors, that you are okay, and you are enough. I am giving you a new Latin motto for your new coat of arms: "*Salveo et satis.*" You are okay and enough to do service, and you are okay and enough to have a successful career as an actor.

10
Your Mountaintop

I originally subtitled this book "How to Be a Successful ~~Actor~~ Acting Person," but then I decided that sounded as if I were trying to be gender nonspecific in a rather preciously politically correct way. What I was aiming for was the idea of the importance of one's success as a whole person. I hope some of the insights and stories I have shared will move you closer to that goal. I sincerely hope that you become a successful actor, but more than that I hope you become a successful person who happens to act.

I am proud to be an actor. I love the process of creating a character. I love the chance to bond with a group of fellow professionals to tell a story. I love to act, and I have been lucky enough to have been paid—and frequently paid well—to practice my craft.

Part of that luck is that my success has enabled me to realize that the key to becoming a successful acting person is not so much the acting as the personhood. Just as the person who thinks that money will bring her happiness inevitably discovers when she gets money that money is not the answer, my success has shown me that financial rewards and juicy roles are not the answer. The answer, if there is *an* answer, has more to do with connecting with other people, making a difference in their lives, being useful, being of service, being a friend, loving someone, loving many someones, loving someone special. You can do all of that without ever getting to act on Broadway or in a feature film or in a network TV show.

So, aim for the Mountaintop of "Successful Acting Person," and Godspeed! I truly hope that you achieve that Mountaintop, that you become a wildly successful actor. But more than the prospect of starring on Broadway or headlining a TV show, I hope that your mosaic brings you joy, that you achieve the goal of becoming a successful person, that you find a satisfying answer to the question of why you are here.

Climb well. Climb safely. Excelsior!

"Louder. Faster. Funnier!"

Index

110 in the Shade, 32
890 Broadway, 96

Abuelita, 134
ACT, 10, 104, 173
Acting Business Boot Camp, 146
Actor Prepares, An, 32
Actors Access, 139–140
Actors and Artists Unite to End
    Alzheimer's, 144
Actors' Equity, 6, 15, 17, 51, 81, 83–84,
    109
AEA, 30, 71, 81
Affordable Care Act, 144
Agency for the Performing Arts, 113
AirBnB, 22
Albany, 17, 160
Allen, Peter, 171
Allen, Woody, 159
allthatchat.com, 86
All the Way, 184
American Musical and Dramatic Academy,
    10
American Academy of Dramatic Arts, 10
American Theatre, 85
André, 170–171
Andrews, George Lee, 29
Angel, 43, 44
Annie, 84
"Anthem," 96
Antigone, 108
Applause, 49
Arena Stage, 20
Asolo, 10
Astoria, 23
Atlanta, 15
audition.cat.com, 47
Aunt Eller, 39
Azenberg, Manny, 172

Backstage, 58, 83–84
Baldwin Wallace, 12
Barnum, 72, 84
Barrington Stage, 10
Barrymore, Drew, 51
Barton, Steve, 170
Beach, Gary, 50, 179
Becker, Leslie, 47
Beckett, Samuel, 142
Behan, Brendan, 150
Berkshire Theatre Festival, 10, 111
Berresse, Michael, 75
Beyoncé, 160
Beyond Therapy, 20
Blanc, Mel, 36
Boston, 22
Boston Conservatory, 10
Boyden, Peter, 36
Brightman, Sarah, 170
Brimstone, 172
"Bring Him Home," 95–96
Bring It On, 84
broadway.com, 85
Broadway Show League, 60
Bronx, 23
Brooklyn, 23–24
Brothers Karamazov, The, 51, 118
Brown, Jason Robert, 74–75
Buchwald, Don, 106
Burbank, 24
Burn This, 50
Burstein, Danny, 163
Buscemi, Steve, 34

CAA, 112, 116
Caddick, David, 171
Call Sheet, 85
Candy, John, 18
Cantzen, Conrad, 83

Career, 19, 172, 177
Carlotta, 170–171
Carnegie Mellon, 10, 11, 28
Carson, Johnny, 123
Cash, 19, 177
Cats, 95
Cat's Cradle, 51
Central School, 11
Century City, 24
CESD, 106
Charles, Keith, 123
Charles River, 5
Chayefsky, Paddy, 184
Chess, 96
Chicago, 4
Church, Forrest, 143
Circle-in-the-Square, 10, 48
City College, 134
Clayburgh, Jill, 169–170
Cloud Nine, 125
Cody, Jen, 42
Columbia, 134
Community, 19, 177
Company, 38
Connet, Bill, 51
Coolidge, Calvin, 146
"Corner of the Sky," 96
Costa Mesa, 24
Count Carl-Magnus, 168
Coverage, 19, 144, 177
Coward, Noel, 150
Cowboy, 44, 59
Craigslist, 22
Cranston, Bryan, 103, 154
Crawford, Michael, 170
Creative, 19, 177, 178
Creativity, 142, 153, 155, 172, 178
Creon, 108
Crucible, The, 42
Cuervo, Alma, 126
Culver City, 24

Daly, Nancy, 144
Davis, Eleanor, 66, 153

Death of a Salesman, 74
DeVito, Danny, 33
Die Hard, 29, 32, 90, 111, 148, 172
DiPietro, Joe, 168
Donovan, Ned, 47
Dossett, John, 179
Douglas, Michael, 170
Doyle, John, 38
Drama Centre, 11
Dukes, David, 41
Durang, Christopher, 20, 51, 118

Ebb, Fred, 4
ECC, 82
Elon, 12
Emerson, 10
Emerson, Michael, 126
Endeavor, 112
Ensemble Studio Theatre, 125
EPA, 82
Equity News, 17, 19
Equity-League, 144
Esper, William, 169
Ethan Frome, 169
Eynsford-Hill, Freddy, 20, 110

Fabergé, 46
Facebook, 11, 135–136, 162
Fantasticks, The, 123
Firmin, 3, 170–171
Fitzgerald, Kathy, 50
Fitzgerald, Scott, 37
Florida, 17
Florida State, 10
Flynn, Billy, 4
Fort Knox, 38
Foster, Jodie, 13
Funny Thing, 41, 43, 45, 48

Gant, Ben, 43–44
Gant, Eugene, 43
Gant, W. O., 43
Garber, Victor, 41
Garcia, Aimee, 157

Garland, Judy, 50
Geld, Gary, 44
General Harrison Howell, 41
Giant, 179
Girl Scouts, 144
Gloriosus, Miles, 41, 43, 45, 110
Godspell, 134
Goldberg, Whoopi, 48
Goodspeed, 44, 166
granfalloon, 51
Granit, Bruce, 169–170
Grease, 54, 84
Greenwich Village, 23–24
Groenendaal, Cris, 45
Groundlings, 35
Guildhall, 11
Gummer, Mamie, 51
Guthrie, 10, 20
Gwenn, Edmund, 35
Gwynne, Fred, 41, 43
Gypsy, 75

Habitat for Humanity, 144
Hair, 60
Hamlet, 42
Handman, Wynn, 60, 157, 169
Hanks, Tom, 87, 163
Harrison, Rex, 20
Harvard, 12, 17, 40–41, 43
Hathaway, Anne, 163
Hayden, Sophie, 72
Hell's Kitchen, 23
Henderson's Casting Directors Guide, 85
Henry V, 42
Herrmann, Ed, 41
Higgins, Henry, 42, 172
Higgins, Joel, 44
Holgate, Ron, 41
Hollywood, 22, 24, 65
Hotel Dixie, 32
Houseman, John, 48
Howard, Ken, 41, 172
Hudson, Rock, 170
Huffman, Cady, 179

In the Heights, 134
Innovative, 106
Instagram, 135–137
Irene, 1
Irons, Jeremy, 90
Ithaca, 10, 12

Javert, 95
Jaws, 169
Jennings, Byron, 126
Jerome, Tim, 172
Jesus Christ Superstar, 60
Jones, Tom, 123
Joslyn, Betsy, 157–158
Jud, 39
Juilliard School, 10, 11, 48, 95
Juliet, 114
Juno's Swans, 125

karass, 44, 51–53, 142–143
Kaye, Judy, 170
Keats, 34
Kelly, Gene, 37
Kerr, Deborah, 86
Kerr, E. Katherine, 125
King, Martin Luther, 160
Kiss Me Kate, 41
Kline, Kevin, 41, 50, 169
Kohlhass, Karen, 90

La Chiusa, Michael John, 172, 179
La Rochefoucauld, 158
LAMDA, 11
Lane, Nathan, 48, 179
Larsen, Liz, 75
Lear, 74
Legs Diamond, 171
Les Misérables, 49, 95, 153, 156
Linville, Larry, 172
Lion King, The, 43
Lipson, Cliff, 59–60
Little Night Music, A, 168
London, 10, 95, 170
Look Homeward Angel, 43

Looney Tunes, 36
Loose Ends, 169–170
LORT, 29, 82, 88
Los Angeles, 15, 20–22, 24
Lycus, Marcus, 43
Lynne, Gillian, 171

Machiavellian, 44–45
Mackintosh, Cameron, 3, 171–172
Magic Show, The, 60, 166
Maine, 16
Malkovich, John, 50
Mamma Mia, 155
Man and Superman, 42
Man Who Came to Dinner, The, 39
Mann, Terry, 95
Mantello, Joe, 118
Manhattan, 23–24
Marinaro, Renata, 145
Martin, Leila, 123
Martin, Steve, 18
M.A.S.H., 172
Matilda, 84
Maugham, Somerset, 158
McCorkle, Pat, 111
McTiernan, John, 111
Mencken, H. L., 67
Merlin, Joanna, 168
Merman, Ethel, 38, 95
Miami, 15
Michigan, 10–11, 82
Mikado, The, 134
Minneapolis, 20
monologueaudition.com, 90
Mordor, 38
My Fair Lady, 20, 172
My Favorite Year, 35

NABET, 106
Network,
Newhart, Chase, 65
New Jersey, 16, 160
New Orleans, 15

New School, the, 134
Newsies, 179
New York, 15–17, 21–23, 111, 123, 163
NoHo Arts District, 24
North Carolina School of the Arts, 10
Northwestern, 10–11
Now Casting, 116, 139
NTI—National Theatre Institute, 10
Nunn, Trevor, 95
NY Film Academy, 134
NYC, 15, 21, 24, 29, 70, 95, 105–106,
      126, 183
NYU, 134
NYU Tisch, 10

O'Brien, Jack, 118
Of Mice and Men, 169
Oklahoma!, 39
Olivier, Laurence, 44
Once, 38
One Flew Over the Cuckoo's Nest, 33
O'Neill Theatre Center, 10
On the Twentieth Century, 50, 169
Oregon Shakespeare Festival, 175–176
Organized Actor, The, 47
Orsino, 20
Osnes, Laura, 163
overnightprints.com, 71

Paper Chase, The, 48
Papp, Joe, 11
Paradigm, 106
Pasadena, 24
Patinkin, Mandy, 95
Perlman, Rhea, 42
Petrified Prince, The, 172
Phantom of the Opera, The, 3, 29, 45,
      153–154, 170–172
Philadelphia, 15
Philemon, 123
Pippin, 75, 84, 96
Pirates of Penzance, 1
Pitti-Sing, 134

Planes, Trains and Automobiles, 18
playbill.com, 85
Players Directory, 116, 139
Point Park University, 10
Polonius, 74
Portman, Natalie, 13
"Prima Donna," 171
Prince, Hal, 168–169
Prince of Broadway, 168–172
Princess Bride, The, 95
Proctor, John, 42
Producers, The, 50, 168, 179
Public Theatre, 172
Pugh, Richard Warren, 153
Pumbaa, 43

Quinn, Patrick, 170

RADA, 11
Raitt, John, 38, 95
Rebecca, 179
Rees, Roger, 10, 126
Reproductions, 70
Richardson, Ralph, 45, 147
Rivals, The, 134
Roberts, Tony, 44
Rogen, Seth, 2
Rose, Peter Pamela, 146
Rose, Philip, 44
Roth, Andy, 92
Royale Theatre, 171
Royal Shakespeare Company, 10
Ruffles, 40
Rumors, 172

Sabella, Ernie, 43
SAG, 106, 116, 139
SAG-AFTRA, 6, 71, 80, 109, 144
Samuel French, 85
Sanders, Jay O., 74
San Fernando Valley, 24
San Francisco, 10, 15, 104
Santa Monica, 24

Schmidt, Harvey, 123
Second City, 35
Seattle, 15, 22
Second Mrs. Wilson, The, 168
senior showcase, 114–115, 133
Shakespeare, 72, 90, 160
shakespeare-monologues.org, 90
Shaw, 90
Sheen, Charlie, 158
Shenandoah, 44
Shenkman, Ben, 126
Show Business, 1–2, 35, 38, 40, 44, 46, 74,
    83–85, 111, 120, 124, 135, 158
Simon, Neil, 172
Singin' in the Rain, 37
site.perfomertrack.com, 47
Snapchat, 135
Sondheim, Stephen, 16, 21, 41, 168
Spring Awakening, 84
St. James Theatre, 48, 169
St. Louis MUNY, 82
Starbuck, 32
Steinkolk, Tess, 64
Stella, Tim, 171
Stiller, Ben, 51
Streep, Meryl, 87, 114
Sue Porter Henderson,
Summerhays, Jane, 37
Sunday in the Park with George,
SUNY Purchase, 10, 74
Surface, Sir Joseph, 134
Sutor, Richard, 61
Sweeney Todd, 38, 42, 168

Tagore, Rabindranath, 143
Tanner, Jack, 42
Targo, Matthias, 111, 148
Taylor, James, 160
Tea and Sympathy, 86
Theatre Communications Group, 85
Theatrical Index, 85
Thenardier, 49, 96, 157
Thurman, Uma, 126

Timon, 43
Tony Award, 160, 169
Trinity Rep, 176
Trinity Rep/Brown, 10
Trump, Donald, 158
Tucker, Robert, 44
Tumblr, 135
Tune, Tommy, 125
Twelfth Night, 20
Twitter, 135–136

Udell, Peter, 44
Un Ballo en Maschera, 171
Unitarian, 32
University of Cincinnati College—
    Conservatory of Music, 10
University of the Arts, 10
Upper West Side, 23–24, 61
Upright Citizens Brigade, 35
Urinetown, 42

Valjean, Jean, 95–96
Very Good Eddie, 32, 40, 59, 166
Vidal, Gore, 158
vistaprint.com, 71
Vo, Tony Aidan, 47

Von Sydow, Max, 41
Vonnegut, Kurt, 51

Walker, Fuschia, 157
Washington, 15, 20, 22
Watson, Emma, 13
Watson, Susan, 123
Webber, Andrew Lloyd, 3, 171
Weill, Claudia, 170
Weller, Michael, 169
Westwood, 21
Whiteside, Sheridan, 39
"Who Am I," 95–96
Whoopee!, 36, 72
Wikipedia, 134
William Morris, 112, 114
Williamstown, 10
Wolfe, Thomas, 43

Yale, 10–11, 40
*You're a Good Man Charlie
    Brown*, 42
YouTube, 135

Zaks, Jerry, 21
Zoo Story, 76

Image Credits

Pages 59, 60: Cliff Lipson Photography. Used by permission.

Pages 61, 62, 63: Photos by Richard and Christiana Sutor. Used by permission.

Page 64: Photos by Tess Steinkolk. Used by permission.

Page 65: Chase Newhart Photography. Used by permission.

Pages 76, 77, 78, 79, 126, 127, 128, 129, 130, 131, 132: Author's collection.

Illustrations on pages 9, 13, 16, 28, 33, 37, 52, 57, 70, 73, 80, 89, 93, 94, 99, 105, 115, 121, 135, 145, 148, 152, 156, 164, 176, 179, and 188 by Michael X. Martin (MXM). All rights reserved. Used by permission.